LITURGY AND ECOLOGY
IN DIALOGUE

LITURGY AND ECOLOGY IN DIALOGUE

Lawrence E. Mick

A Liturgical Press Book

THE LITURGICAL PRESS
Collegeville, Minnesota

Cover design by Greg Becker

Manufactured in the United States of America.

1   2   3   4   5   6   7   8   9

Library of Congress Cataloging-in-Publication Data

Mick, Lawrence E., 1946–
   Liturgy and ecology in dialogue / by Lawrence E. Mick.
      p.   cm.
   Includes bibliographical references.
   ISBN 0-8146-2447-2
   1. Catholic Church—Liturgy. 2. Human ecology—Religious aspects—Catholic Church.   I. Title.
 BX1970.M517   1997
 261.8'362—dc21   97–956
                                                          CIP

Contents

Introduction

More than twenty years ago I wrote an article on ecology and worship for *Pastoral Life* magazine (November 1972), in which I tried to briefly articulate some of the connections between the growing ecological movement and the still young liturgical renewal mandated by the Second Vatican Council. Since that time there has been considerable growth in both movements. The development of ecological awareness in the United States has been called the "greening" of America; a similar heightened awareness can be noted throughout the world, expressed most clearly in the international Earth Summit held in Brazil in June 1992. Slowly but steadily people all around the globe are becoming more aware of the need to protect and preserve the natural environment from the devastating effects of human abuse and degradation.

The liturgical movement in the Catholic Church has also progressed significantly in the past quarter-century, and similar change can be noted in many Protestant communities as well. The fruit of decades of scholarly research has been blended with a strong pastoral concern for spiritual growth to enable Christians of various denominations to engage in more lively and more beautiful worship of the Lord.

At the same time, it must be admitted that we still have a long way to go. The gains in ecological awareness have not been enfleshed in concrete action and changed lifestyles on a scale broad enough to reverse the pattern of ecological devastation that has accompanied modern technological developments. There are still far too many people who do not see the care of creation as their own responsibility, and even those who do accept the responsibility find that seeing the problem and solving the problem are two different things. Changes in personal lifestyle are painful to implement, and changes in corporate and government policies require long battles with powerful and entrenched interests to achieve even minimal progress.

In a similar way, the liturgical renewal has also seen uneven progress. Few worshiping communities experience lively worship on a regular basis. While many parishes have made progress in training liturgical ministers, others are still content with mediocre ministry. Preaching has improved in the Catholic community, but parishioners still see this as a major weakness. The musical repertoire has broadened and matured, yet competent music ministers are still rare in Catholic parishes, and just salaries are even more unusual. More people are involved in various ministries in the liturgy, yet the involvement of the most basic ministers, the assembly itself, is generally half-hearted at best.

My first book, *To Live as We Worship* (The Liturgical Press, 1984) was based on the fundamental premise that what we do in worship should have a profound effect on all the other areas of our lives. There should be no gap between liturgy and life, for liturgy expresses the very meaning of our lives. This book flows from that same conviction. A deeper ecological awareness has valuable links to a better liturgical practice.

Moreover, the benefits flow in both directions. Worshiping communities would benefit from more attention paid to the actual environment in which liturgy takes place as well as from a deeper respect for the many facets of creation that are part of our sacramental life. At the same time, the ecological movement can benefit from the positive effect that worship should have on those who enter into it.

The aim of this book is to explore those bidirectional links to see how both worship and our ecological awareness can be improved by attention to both sides of the connection. We will examine how worship might help us develop a deeper awareness of ecological issues and also how a stronger ecological mind-set might help us improve our worship.

The fundamental basis of ecological awareness is the interconnected nature of all things in the universe. The movement grows out of a deepening recognition of the essential bonds between all elements of creation. These connections may be most obvious among the living members of a given ecological community. We have learned that removing one species from such a community often drastically alters the whole life chain that connected a variety of species of living things. Gradually we have also become aware that no ecological niche is self-contained and that both living and non-living elements are linked in ever-widening circles, eventually encompassing the whole earth and even the wider universe.

In a similar way, those who work with the worship of the Church have learned that no worship experience and no worshiping community are self-contained. All parts of the lives of those who worship are linked, and it is often nonliturgical issues that support or obstruct good liturgy. The more those who prepare worship are aware of the connections that do exist, and that should exist, between worship and the rest of the lives of those who make up the assembly, the better they will be at facilitating lively and prayerful worship. Both worship and ecology require a strong sense of the connectedness of all things in life.

But the links between worship and ecology are much deeper than the general interconnectedness of creation and human life. The core of the distinctiveness of Christianity itself is its belief in the incarnation—its belief that the Son of God took on human flesh and lived among us. This doctrine undergirds the sacramental economy of the Church, for it recognizes that God may be met in the human and in the created. Our sacramental worship uses water, oil, bread, wine, wood, flowers, incense, human words, and human touch. Through these human and created things we seek to encounter our God, and our use of these gifts of creation should engender a respect for all God's creation, a respect that provides an essential basis for the whole ecological movement.

Thus worship and ecology are bound together at their core, in their common recognition of creation as a gift to be cherished and not abused. This book will seek to expand the reader's awareness of how intimately these two movements of our time are linked to each other and how powerfully they can help each other to achieve their respective goals.

At the outset, we should also note the limits of this endeavor. I am a liturgist, not a scientist, so I will not break any new ground in ecological science. I hope rather to assemble enough information on the ecological issues facing us today to give an adequate picture of both the problem and the potential for improvement. I am also a Roman Catholic, so my perspective on worship flows from that tradition. I am convinced that all Christian worship shares many fundamental themes and elements, so much that is discussed here should apply beyond the Roman Catholic communion, but I will not attempt to explicate those applications beyond my own denomination. I am also aware that non-Christian worship shares many elements with Christian liturgy and perhaps is often more in tune with creation than many Christians have been. The scope of this work will not allow much treatment of those links either.

Despite these necessary limitations, however, I hope that this book will be useful to all those who care about our environment and all those who worship the one God who created it all. The following chapters represent a kind of extended meditation on the various ways that our worship and our concern for the environment intersect. May it prompt your own reflections, prayer, and action.

Chapter One

Ecology as a Moral Issue

Many people have heard the story of the farmer who was out in his field one day when a neighbor was passing by. Being a devout man, the neighbor commented that the Lord and the farmer had created a beautiful field. "Yes," replied the farmer, "and you should have seen it when the Lord had it all to himself!"

Human impact on the natural environment is as old as the human race. Frequently the impact is positive, as humans function as co-creators, adding human creativity to God's fundamental creative act. Often, however, the impact has not been positive. The planet today still shows the scars of ancient degradation of the environment. North Africa, once the breadbasket of the Roman Empire, is now largely desert, with ancient cities covered by drifting sand. Overgrazing, lumbering, and poor farming practices caused the loss of topsoil and the eventual desertification of the land. The Sahara continues to advance southward every year in our own time due largely to similar violations of the natural order. In the Middle East, the Fertile Crescent of biblical times is also mostly desert today. The modern state of Israel has had some spectacular success at reclaiming sections of desert land by irrigation, but this is a pale echo of the region's fertile past. Most of the forests in China were cut down long ago as well.

In more recent eras, our own continent has lost all but a small percentage of the forests that once spanned from ocean to ocean, and the Great Plains were plowed and farmed with little regard for ecological preservation. The Dust Bowl of the

1930s began to wake up the country to the devastation caused by poor farming and grazing practices, yet we continue to lose vast amounts of topsoil each year because of erosive farming practices. The growth of agribusiness in recent years has only accelerated the devastation as short-term profits take precedence over long-term sustainability.

Much of this devastation is the result of an attitude that the land and all of nonhuman creation is there for the taking. Natural resources are exploited for human profit, regardless of the consequences for the future. Some of the exploiters in past ages could have used ignorance as an excuse, since the complex interconnection in ecological communities was not as fully understood as it is today. Current exploitation of the environment, however, must be attributed to greed and willful ignoring of the consequences.

Some have sought to place the blame directly on Judaism and Christianity, claiming that pagan religions were more respectful of creation than was the Judeo-Christian vision of humans as the masters of creation. The classic text blamed for this view is in the book of Genesis: "Be fertile and multiply; fill the earth and subdue it. Have dominion over the fish of the sea, the birds of the air, and all the living things that move on the earth" (Gen 1:28).

Whether there is a real basis for blame in this text is a debatable question. Judaism and Christianity also have very positive perspectives on creation as belonging to God and on humanity's role as steward of that creation. In any case, placing blame for past errors is not all that helpful; what is needed is a commitment to care for the environment in the future. Christianity has the potential to support such efforts as well as any other religion does.

Native American Spirituality

Undoubtedly there is much that we can learn from non-Christian perspectives, most notably that of the Native American people. While there is danger of an overly romantic view of the Native Americans living in harmony with creation, it is fairly clear that they did live in closer harmony with the animal and plant world than many of their European conquerors did. They lived on this continent for many centuries with no drastic changes in the ecology of the land. As a whole, they lived rather lightly upon the land, in general harmony with the plant and animal communities that abounded here and provided them with food, clothing, shelter, medicine, and other necessities.

An eloquent expression of the Native American perspective is found in a letter written in 1854 to President Franklin Pierce and commonly attributed to Chief Seattle of the Duwamish tribe. It is worth quoting extensively here:

> The President in Washington sends word that he wishes to buy our land. But how can you buy or sell the sky? The land? The idea is strange to us. If we do not own the freshness of the air and the sparkle of the water, how can you buy them?
>
> Every part of this earth is sacred to my people. Every shiny pine needle, every sandy shore, every mist in the dark woods, every meadow, every humming insect. All are holy in the memory and experience of my people.
>
> We know the sap which courses through the trees as we know the blood that courses through our veins. We are part of the earth and it is part of us. The perfumed flowers are our sisters. The bear, the deer, the great eagle, these are our brothers. The rocky crests, the juices in the meadow, the body heat of the pony, and man, all belong to the same family.
>
> The rivers are our brothers. They quench our thirst. They carry our canoes and feed our children. So you must give to the rivers the kindness you would give any brother.
>
> If we sell you our land, remember that the air is precious to us, that the air shares its spirit with all the life it supports. The wind that gave our grandfather his first breath also receives his last sigh. The wind also gives our children the spirit of life. So if we sell you our land, you must keep it apart and sacred, as a place where man can go to taste the wind that is sweetened by the meadow flowers.
>
> Will you teach your children what we have taught our children? That the earth is our mother? What befalls the earth befalls all the sons of the earth.
>
> This we know: the earth does not belong to man, man belongs to the earth. All things are connected like the blood that unites us all. Man did not weave the web of life, he is merely a strand in it. Whatever he does to the web, he does to himself.

One thing we know: our god is also your god. The earth is precious to him and to harm the earth is to heap contempt on its creator.

We know that the white man does not understand our ways. One portion of the land is the same to him as the next, for he is a stranger who comes in the night and takes from the land whatever he needs. The earth is not his brother but his enemy, and when he has conquered it, he moves on. He leaves his fathers' graves and his children's birthplace is forgotten.

There is no quiet place in the white man's cities. No place to hear the leaves of spring or the rustle of insect wings. But perhaps because I am savage and do not understand—the clatter only seems to insult the ears. And what is there to life if a man cannot hear the lovely cry of the whippoorwill or the arguments of the frog around the pond at night?

The whites, too, shall pass—perhaps faster than the tribes. Continue to contaminate your bed and you will one night suffocate in your waste. When the buffalo are all slaughtered, the wild horses all tamed, the secret corners of the forest heavy with the scent of many men, and the view of the ripe hills blotted out by talking wires. Where is the thicket? Gone. Where is the eagle? Gone. And what is it to say good-bye to the swift and the hunt, the end of the living and the beginning of survival?[1]

This letter summarizes quite well the Native Americans' experience of the sacredness of all living and nonliving things on the earth. It speaks clearly of their sense of kinship with all living creatures and with the earth and sky and water as well. It expresses the sense of wonder and awe that the natural world evokes and the respect and reverence that guided their relations with the rest of creation.

Recovering Our Tradition

Such respect and reverence, however, are not unique to Native American spirituality. While it is true that some Christians through the ages have interpreted the gift of dominion over creation as a justification for the abuse of creation by humans, it is also true that our own tradition offers ex-

1. Quoted in *Maryknoll* 84:1 (Jan. 1990) 59–62 and in Joseph Campbell, *The Power of Myth* (New York: Doubleday, 1988) 34.

amples of a much more positive approach to the environment in which we live.

The Hebrew Scriptures offer numerous examples that present creation as God's throne (and thus deserving respect) and as God's gift to humanity (and thus to be treasured). The psalms include texts praising God for creation (e.g., Psalm 104) and calling on all parts of creation to join in praise to their Creator and Lord (e.g., Psalm 148). The earth is seen as belonging to God (e.g., Psalm 24) and only entrusted to humanity for its use. Humans are to be stewards of creation and are expected to use it according to God's will. The tradition of sacrifices among the Israelites also testifies to the recognition that all creation ultimately belongs to God.

In the Christian Scriptures, too, creation is not despised but treasured. Jesus frequently uses images from the natural world in his parables and evidences a comfortable closeness to nature in his own lifestyle. One of the most intriguing biblical perspectives on creation is found in Paul's letter to the Romans:

> For creation waits with eager expectation the revelation of the children of God; for creation was made subject to futility, not of its own accord but because of the one who subjected it, in hope that creation itself would be set free from slavery to corruption and share in the glorious freedom of the children of God. We know that all creation is groaning in labor pains even until now; and not only that, but we ourselves, who have the first-fruits of the Spirit, we also groan within ourselves as we wait for adoption, the redemption of our bodies (Rom 8:19-23).

This text has a strong basis in the Jewish tradition. Genesis 3:17 sees the curse of the earth as a result of human sin. The covenant with Noah in Genesis 9:8-17 embraces all creation. And Isaiah 65:17, among other passages, speaks of a new heaven and a new earth in the time of the fulfillment of divine promises. This passage from Romans links the future of creation itself to the future of the children of God, looking toward the redemption of all of creation, not just of human beings. While the passage is not as clear as we might wish about what that redemption will entail, it certainly suggests a deep reverence for all creation, which is to share in the glorious freedom of God's children.

Paul returns to this same theme of the restoration of all things in Christ in Colossians 1:15-20 and Ephesians 1:9-10, 22-23:

> He is the image of the invisible God,
>   the firstborn of all creation.
> For in him were created all things in heaven and on earth,
>   the visible and the invisible,
>   whether thrones or dominions or principalities or powers;
>   all things were created through him and for him.
> He is before all things,
>   and in him all things hold together.
> He is the head of the body, the church.
>   He is the beginning, the firstborn from the dead,
>   that in all things he himself might be preeminent.
> For in him all the fullness was pleased to dwell,
>   and through him to reconcile all things for him,
>   making peace by the blood of his cross [through him],
>   whether those on earth or those in heaven (Col 1:15-20).

> [God] has made known to us the mystery of his will in accord with his favor that he set forth in him as a plan for the fullness of times, to sum up all things in Christ, in heaven and on earth (Eph 1:9-10).

> And he put all things beneath his feet and gave him as head over all things to the church, which is his body, the fullness of the one who fills all things in every way (Eph 1:22-23).

These passages make it clear that Paul saw Christ as the Lord of the whole universe and that redemption in Christ involves not only human beings but all things, which were created through Christ, in whom all things hold together. This is a somewhat neglected aspect of the Christian tradition, but Paul's vision offers a strong foundation for a Christian ecological awareness.

Christian Witnesses

In the history of Christianity, several other figures stand out for their positive valuation of creation. Perhaps the best known is St. Francis of Assisi. This thirteenth-century preacher of the gospel lived close to the earth and saw creation as his brothers and sisters. He is said to have preached to the birds, to have befriended a dangerous wolf, and to have used live animals around a manger to celebrate Christmas. His ecological awareness is perhaps best expressed in his Canticle to the Sun, in which he sings to Brother Sun, Sister Moon, Brother Wind, Sister Water, Brother Fire, and Mother Earth, praising God for the gifts of creation. His language is remarkably similar to that of the letter from Chief Seattle quoted above. St. Francis was proclaimed the patron saint of ecology by Pope John Paul II in 1979.

In the same historical period, the writings of the mystic Meister Eckhart also reflect the importance of a creation consciousness. Several other mystical writers of that era also stressed the presence of God in creation, including Hildegard of Bingen, Mechtild of Magdeburg, and Julian of Norwich.

In our own century, the writings of the Jesuit theologian Pierre Teilhard de Chardin, the Trappist monk Thomas Merton, and the Dominican Matthew Fox all witness in different ways to this same thread in the Christian tradition. Teilhard combined geology, paleontology, philosophy, and theology in a vision that sees all creation evolving to a spiritual synthesis. Merton says that humans find their true selves only in communion with the true God, and in that communion one is also united with all persons and with all creatures in God's creation. Fox has developed a whole school of "creation spirituality"; while there are some questions about particular points of his teaching, there is no question that he has helped many Christians, Catholic and Protestant, to recover creation insights from Christian and Jewish sources. There is much to be gained from other traditions in learning to value creation properly, but it is important for Christians also to rediscover these same insights in our own tradition.

The Writings of Pope John Paul II

In several of his writings, Pope John Paul II has raised ecological concerns as matters of moral responsibility. In his 1981 encyclical *On Human Work (Laborem Exercens)*, he presents human work as a sharing in the activity of the Creator and quotes the Second Vatican Council's Dogmatic Constitution on the Church (*Lumen Gentium*, no. 36): "The faithful, therefore, must learn the deepest meaning and the value of all creation, and its orientation to the praise of God."[2] In his encyclical *The Redeemer of Man (Redemptor Hominis*, March 4, 1979), Pope John Paul insists that "it was the Creator's will that [we] should communicate with nature as an intelligent and noble *master* and *guardian*, and not as a heedless *exploiter* and *destroyer.*"[3]

Pope John Paul's theme for the World Day of Peace in 1990 was "Peace with God the Creator; Peace with All of Creation." In his message for that observance, he insisted that the "ecological crisis is a moral issue. . . . Respect for life and for the dignity of the human person extends also to the rest of creation. . . ."[4] And in his encyclical *On the Hundredth Anniversary of Rerum Novarum (Centesimus Annus)*, he raises the ecological question clearly as a moral question:

> Man thinks that he can make arbitrary use of the earth, sub-jecting it without restraint to his will, as though it did not have its own requisites and a prior God-given purpose, which man can indeed develop but must not betray. Instead of carrying out his role as a cooperator with God in the work of creation, man sets himself up in place of God and thus ends up provoking a rebellion on the part of nature.[5]

In his encyclical *The Gospel of Life (Evangelium Vitae)*, the pontiff again addressed ecological concerns:

> As one called to till and look after the garden of the world (cf. Gen. 2:15), man has a specific responsibility towards the environment in which he lives, towards the creation which God has put at the service of his personal dignity, of his life, not only for the present but also for future generations. It is the ecological question—ranging from the preservation of natural habitats of

2. *On Human Work* (Washington: United States Catholic Conference, 1981) no. 25.

3. *The Redeemer of Man* (Washington: United States Catholic Conference, 1979) no. 15.

4. *The Pope Speaks*, vol. 35, no. 3 (May–June 1990) 206.

5. *On the Hundredth Anniversary of Rerum Novarum* (Washington: United States Catholic Conference, 1991) no. 37.

the different species of animals and of other forms of life to "human ecology" properly speaking—which finds in the Bible clear and strong ethical direction, leading to a solution which respects the great good of life, of every life.[6]

The United States Bishops' Pastoral Letter

The United States Catholic bishops, in their pastoral letter on the economy, offer some seminal statements about the proper Christian approach to creation. They view creation from a biblical perspective, beginning with the book of Genesis. The bishops note that Genesis calls creation "very good" and suggest that the creation stories in Genesis lead to a conviction that every dimension of human life is under God's care. They add that "God is present to creation, and creative engagement with God's handiwork is itself reverence for God." The bishops note that "men and women are also to share in the creative activity of God," and "are to be faithful stewards in caring for the earth." Summarizing the history of our faith, they state that "from the patristic period to the present, the church has affirmed that misuse of the world's resources or appropriation of them by a minority of the world's population betrays the gift of creation since 'whatever belongs to God belongs to all.'"[7]

The Philippine Bishops' Pastoral Letter

A number of other statements have been issued by various bishops' conferences throughout the world, including *The Ecological Crisis* by the Federation of Asian Bishops' Conferences (1989); *Ecology: The Bishops of Lombardy Address the Community* by the bishops of northern Italy (1989); and *Crying Out for the Land* by the Bishops' Conference of Guatemala (1988).

One of the most eloquent statements is a pastoral letter issued by the Catholic bishops of the Philippines in 1988 entitled

6. *The Gospel of Life* (Washington: United States Catholic Conference, 1995) no. 42.

7. *Economic Justice for All: Pastoral Letter on Catholic Social Teaching and the U.S. Economy* (Washington: National Conference of Catholic Bishops, 1986) nos. 31, 32, 34.

What Is Happening to Our Beautiful Land? In this reflection on ecological destruction, they present ecology as a fundamental pro-life issue, noting that the ecological crisis is the root of many of the economic and political problems facing that island nation. They state clearly that this "assault on creation is sinful and contrary to the teachings of our faith." This conviction flows in part from their recognition that destruction of the environment leads to unjust situations for the poor, but it is also based on a recognition of Christ as "the center point of human history and creation." They insist that "the destruction of any part of creation, especially the extinction of species, defaces the image of Christ, which is etched in creation."[8]

Pollution as Sin

In a similar vein, a statement by Lutheran theologian Joseph Sittler has often been quoted: "Reason says that destroying clean air is impractical; faith ought to say it is blasphemous."[9] Sittler's 1959 Beecher lectures at Yale University were entitled "The Ecology of Faith," and he was one of the first theologians in this century to bring together ecology and theology. As the quotations above have shown, however, he was not the last. There is a growing recognition that care of the environment is a moral obligation and that pollution and other forms of environmental degradation are sinful.

The nature of the sin in such cases may be viewed from various perspectives. Mistreatment of the environment is a rejection or misuse of God's gifts to the human race. Because these gifts are meant for all, such misuse is also a sin against justice and against charity. Environmental destruction is frequently the result of greed and selfishness. And defacing creation mars the image of God reflected there. All these perspectives combine to lead to the conclusion that ecology is not

8. "What Is Happening to Our Beautiful Land?" SEDOS (Service of Documentation and Study) no. 4 (April 15, 1988) 112–115. See also *"And God Saw that It Was Good": Catholic Theology and the Environment*, ed. Drew Christiansen and Walter Grazier (Washington: United States Catholic Conference, 1996) 309–318.

9. Quoted in *Christopher News Notes*, no. 322, Feb. 1990.

just a social or political or economic question but a profoundly moral issue.

Sin and Forgiveness

Moral issues have always been a major part of Christian teaching and living and sacraments. In particular, the Catholic Church has continually insisted on the need for repentance and continuing conversion, turning away from sin and turning more fully to God. The sacrament of reconciliation is the most obvious expression of this belief, but it is not the only one. Baptism is celebrated "for the remission of sin," and every Eucharist proclaims Christ's triumph over sin through his death and resurrection. The penitential rite at the beginning of Mass and the sign of peace also attest to the continual human need for forgiveness and reconciliation. All the sacraments, in various ways, call for continuing conversion to Christ as the fundamental life task of every Christian.

In contemporary American culture, it is considered a bit gauche to speak of sin. Anything that is wrong with any person must have its source outside the person. Parents or society or poverty or sexual abuse in childhood or racism is to blame. Yet with all the blame that is assigned to others, there seems to be a great reluctance to call the sources of disorder, wherever they are located, by the name of sin. Even rarer is the ability to recognize blame in oneself and to take personal responsibility for one's actions.

The liturgy has no such qualms. In the midst of worship, we are frequently invited to admit our sinfulness and to recognize our need for forgiveness. We celebrate God's great mercy, and in the light of the divine generosity in forgiving, we are set free to admit our need for healing, not because someone else made us do evil things, but because evil is part of our lives and finds a home in our hearts.

Until we are willing to recognize the sins that are involved in environmental destruction, we will have a very hard time confronting the evil that leads to this degradation of the environment. Every action that harms the ecology of the planet is ultimately a personal decision, and every decision is either in accord with or in violation of the will of God. Every decision human beings make is a moral decision; it is either an act of virtue or a sinful act.

Many of the human decisions and actions that degrade the environment are properly called sins. To pollute the air and water is a sin against the Creator and against all those who have a right to clean air and water. To contaminate the land with toxic chemicals is a sin against creation and against all those whose food comes from the land. To adopt farming practices that cause unnecessary erosion, to waste natural resources, to dump garbage in the oceans, and even to throw litter on the roadside and in the wilderness are all sinful actions.

So, too, sins of omission harm the environment: not recycling, not making provision for toxic and radioactive waste, not disposing of household chemicals properly, not voting for laws that will protect the environment. Our society needs to face honestly the sinfulness of the many ways we damage the environment. We need to ask for forgiveness and resolve not to continue living in this sinful manner.

The *Catechism of the Catholic Church* links ecological issues to the seventh commandment:

> The seventh commandment enjoins respect for the integrity of creation. Animals, like plants and inanimate beings, are by nature destined for the common good of past, present, and future humanity. Use of the mineral, vegetable, and animal resources of the universe cannot be divorced from respect for moral imperatives. Man's dominion over inanimate and other living beings granted by the Creator is not absolute; it is limited by concern for the quality of life of his neighbor, including generations to come; it requires a religious respect for the integrity of creation.[10]

When we learn to call sin by its true name and face the guilt of our actions, then we can begin to change our patterns of behavior and convert our lives to bring them into harmony with God's will and thus into harmony with all of God's creation. Allowing the liturgy to shape our recognition of the real-

10. *Catechism of the Catholic Church* (Washington: United States Catholic Conference, 1994) no. 2415.

ity of evil within us as well as around us and learning to trust God's forgiving love will enable us to be more honest about our sins against creation and against others who have a right to share in the goods of creation.

Love of God and Neighbor

Ultimately, a Christian approach to ecology is based on the dual commandment of Christ: we are called to love God above all things and to love our neighbor as ourselves. Love of God requires respect for God's gifts and for God's will for creation, and love of neighbor requires justice, which prohibits selfish destruction of the environment without regard for those in need today or for the needs of future generations.

Recognition of the importance of the religious basis for the ecological movement has grown gradually in recent decades. For example, Vice-President Albert Gore (then senator from Tennessee), speaking to the Forum on Global Change and Our Common Future at the National Academy of Sciences in 1989, insisted that the ecological problem "cannot be solved without reference to spiritual values found in every faith."[11]

Religious involvement in the first Earth Day in 1970 was not evident at all, but Dennis Hayes, the organizer of Earth Day in 1990, called for religious participation to be an integral part of the observance. On August 28, 1993, the Churchwide Assembly of the Evangelical Lutheran Church in America passed a social teaching statement titled "Caring for Creation: Vision, Hope, and Justice" and dealing with ecology issues. On October 4, 1993 (the feast of St. Francis of Assisi), Vice-President Gore joined leaders of several major Christian and Jewish organizations to launch the National Religious Partnership for the Environment to foster grassroots activities for environmental justice in congregations across the country.

A number of statements on ecology have been issued by various Christian denominations in recent years, including the Lutheran Church, Missouri Synod (1992), the United Methodist Church (1988, 1992), the Church of the Brethren (1991), the

11. "Come In, Planet Earth, Are You Listening?" in *Bibelot*, vol. 4, nos. 4, 5, 6 (Dayton: United Theological Seminary, 1989) 17.

Episcopal Church (1991), the American Baptist Churches (1990), the Presbyterian Church (1990), the Greek Orthodox Archdiocese of North and South America (1990), the United Church of Christ (1990), the Mennonite Church (1989), and the Reformed Church in America (1982). Several statements have also been issued by the World Council of Churches in the past decade. A five-part document known as the Assisi Declaration (1986) addresses ecological concerns from Buddhist, Christian, Hindu, Jewish, and Moslem perspectives. These and other recent events indicate a growing awareness of the religious implications of the ecological crisis and the growing involvement of religious bodies in responding to the problem.

Questions for Reflection and Discussion

1. As you look around the area in which you live, what evidences of human impact on the environment are most obvious to you? Are they positive or negative influences?

2. How much respect for creation do you find in the Jewish and Christian Scriptures? Do you see all creation as involved in Christ's redemption? Are there historical figures in the Judeo-Christian tradition that help you develop a deeper care for the environment?

3. Are Native American perspectives helpful to you in deepening your own ecological awareness? Why or why not?

4. Were you familiar with statements of the Pope and national bishops' conferences about the environment? How can this kind of teaching be shared more effectively with your parish?

5. Do you see your work as a sharing in God's creative activity? What about parenting, household tasks, or art and craft projects? In what ways are you a co-creator with God?

6. Do you see ecological issues as moral issues? Have you ever heard environmental damage described as sin? Have you ever felt a need to confess sins against the environment in the sacrament of penance?

7. Is love of God and neighbor an effective base for ecological decisions? Can you name some specific environmental decisions or situations that either support or violate this foundation?

8. How involved is your parish in the environmental movement? What parish organizations might spearhead such involvement? Where can you begin?

Chapter Two

The Interconnectedness
of All Things

Hyperindividualism vs. Community

Someone once asked the philosopher David Hume what he considered to be the object of good legislation. "The greatest good to the greatest number," he replied. "And what," he was asked, "do you consider the greatest number?" His answer: "Number one." Such a response will find many echoes in contemporary society. We are well-trained to look out for "number one." The problem is that we have tended to forget that "number one" is part of a much larger community, and their futures are inextricably linked.

A fundamental principle of ecology is the interconnectedness of all creation. Recognition of this interconnectedness is what has been often lacking in the decisions and actions that have devastated the environment. Recent research has continually revealed how thoroughly interconnected all parts of creation really are. We are increasingly aware of the ripple effects of almost everything we do within our ecological communities.

We are becoming more aware, too, that ecological problems are not just local but often global in scope. Acid rain destroys forests in New England and Canada because of smokestack emissions in the Midwest. The nuclear disaster at Chernobyl sent clouds of radioactivity around the globe. Changes in ocean temperatures in the South Pacific affect weather patterns all across North America and beyond.

Garbage dumped into the sea washes up on beaches far from the site of the dumping. The declining population of songbirds in New York State results from the loss of their winter homes in South America as the tropical forests are destroyed.

This growing awareness of interconnectedness, however, often meets opposition in our Western culture, and particularly in American culture. At least since the Enlightenment, Western society has placed increasing value on the individual. While this is a positive development in many ways, it tends to diminish our awareness of the community and our links to others. The United States has exalted the individual to great heights. It is safe to say that no other civilization in the history of the human race has placed so much value on individual freedom or protected so fully the rights of the individual. This is a gift we have given to the world, and we rightly hope that respect for individual freedom and rights will continue to spread among all peoples.

But every strength contains its own weakness, and our stress on individual freedom has led to such an emphasis on the individual that we have almost forgotten that we have a need for and obligations to the community. Communal thinking is hard for most Americans, and the stress on extreme individualism seems to have reached a high point in recent decades. It has led us to widespread selfishness, glorified by politicians and business leaders and the media. "What's in it for me?" has become the primary criterion by which we judge everything. Politics has become largely a matter of narrow interest groups fighting for their own personal agendas, while citizens are urged to vote based solely on their own pocketbook or personal fears. Seldom is there even any mention of the common good, much less a willingness to sacrifice one's personal interest in favor of the needs of the community.

Progress in the ecological movement requires a concern for the common good, a concern that must be recovered in our private and public thinking in this country. Concern for the common good requires sacrifice from individuals. It limits the desires of the individual in light of the needs of all. It does not allow greed and selfishness to reign supreme. Our sense of interconnectedness with all creation must include a strong awareness of our connections with all human beings. Ultimately, of course, concern for the common good is good for the individual, too. If we destroy the environment, the effects touch the polluter as well as others. But short-term greed has too often won out over the long-term good.

Private Property and Common Heritage

One area that reflects our lack of awareness of our interconnectedness is our use of private property. We need to balance our sense of ownership with a sense of stewardship, our view of private property with a view of the earth as our common heritage. As Aldo Leopold put it: "We abuse land because we regard it as a commodity belonging to us. When we see land as a community to which we belong, we may begin to use it with love and respect. That land is a community is the basic concept of ecology, but that land is to be loved and respected is an extension of ethics"[1] We might add that seeing the land as the common resource of the whole human race would also change our approach to its use and abuse.

Jonathan Helfand tells the Talmudic story of a farmer who was tossing stones from his field onto the public road. A pious man asked him why he was clearing stones from land that was not his and putting them on land that was his. The farmer scoffed at this strange logic. Later he had to sell his farm. As he walked on the public road, he fell on the same stones he had deposited there. He then understood that damage to the public domain is also damage to his own well-being.[2] We need to increase our awareness of how thoroughly our own personal future is linked to the well-being of the whole human race and, in fact, the well-being of the whole planet.

Anthropological Hubris vs. Integration

A lion was once walking proudly through the jungle when he met a monkey. The lion roared and asked the mon-

1. *A Sand County Almanac* (New York: Ballantine Books, 1966) xviii–xix.

2. "The Earth Is the Lord's: Judaism and Environmental Ethics," *Religion and Environmental Crisis,* ed. Eugene Hargrove (Athens, Ga.: Univ. of Georgia Press, 1986) 49.

key, "Who is the king of the jungle?" The frightened monkey replied, "You are, O mighty one." And the lion regally walked on. Later he came upon a zebra. He roared again and asked "Who is the king of the jungle?" "Clearly, you are, O regal one," answered the zebra. The lion smiled and continued on. Soon he came upon an elephant, roared, and asked the same question. Without a word, the elephant grabbed him with his trunk, twirled him around and threw him across the clearing. The lion picked himself up, snorted, and said "Just because you don't know the answer is no reason to get upset!"

Often we humans have moved through our world in a similar manner, believing that we were royalty who could do as we pleased. Moving from a sense of absolute ownership to a recognition of our role as stewards requires a certain amount of humility. One of the roots of past ecological devastation is the arrogance of humans toward the rest of creation. When we view ourselves as masters dominating creation and using it or abusing it at our pleasure, we wreak havoc.

Recognition of God as the true master of creation and ourselves as stewards enables us to begin to see our role in an integrated view of the universe. We are not masters above creation but servants within creation. We have a special role, but it is one that gives us greater responsibility to care for creation, not the right to destroy it. We need to learn to see ourselves as one part of a larger whole and to recognize that our own well-being depends on our care of the ecological web of which we are a part.

The humility needed for this perspective is an integral part of liturgical worship. In worship we explicitly express our recognition of God as the source and master of all creation, including ourselves. We are not self-made persons, and in worship we acknowledge our debt to our Creator. We admit our sinfulness and ask forgiveness for our prideful actions. We give thanks to God for the gifts of creation, and such gratitude engenders respect for the gifts. Worship offers a constant antidote to the kind of hubris that leads to ecological disasters.

The Need for Global Cooperation

Seeing ourselves as part of the whole ecological web quickly leads us to recognize the global nature of the ecological crisis and the need for global cooperation in caring for the environment. Here, too, the worship life of Christians offers assistance. Since in liturgy we celebrate the redemption of the world through the death and resurrection of Christ, we are constantly called to a global perspective. One of the fundamental dynamics of the Christian message is a constantly widening circle of inclusion. Worship calls us into a community to celebrate together and sends us forth into the wider community to spread the love of Christ to all.

Despite frequent efforts to limit the good news of the gospel to those of our own kind, a constant recourse to the word of God in worship continually challenges any such limited worldviews and calls us to a global concern. It is not accidental that the Church calls itself "catholic." The word means "universal," and it should remind us always that salvation is intended for all people. To be truly catholic, we need to nurture a global perspective.

In his last speech as ambassador to the United Nations, Adlai Stevenson expressed a global viewpoint in picturesque fashion: "We travel together, passengers on a little spaceship, dependent on its vulnerable resources of air and soil; all committed for our safety to its security and peace; preserved from annihilation only by the care, the work, and, I will say, the love we give our fragile craft."[3] Many others have made similar comments, urging recognition of our common destiny on this limited planet.

A Pale Blue Dot

This view of the earth as a unified body was reinforced for people all over the world by the pictures sent back from the Apollo space missions to the moon. Seeing the earth as a beautiful blue-green orb in the vast darkness of space gave the world a strong symbol of our unity and our common destiny. Those who care about liturgy know the power of a symbol to express the deepest meanings of our lives. This symbol stands as a constant reminder of our connectedness and of our need

3. *The Papers of Adlai Stevenson*, vol. 8, ed. Walter Johnson (Boston: Little, Brown & Company, 1979) 828.

for global awareness and global cooperation to care for our common home.

Other pictures taken from Voyager I from 3.7 billion miles from earth show our home planet as a pale blue dot in a vast cosmic sea of space. We are reminded by such perspectives of our place in a much bigger universe; perhaps we are prodded by them to have a bit more humility as well.

The Earth as a Living Organism

Some in the ecological movement have gone beyond a sense of common destiny and interconnectedness to suggest that we should view the earth itself as a living organism. The name of an ancient goddess of the earth, Gaia, has been used to denote the earth as a living being. Within this organism a variety of life systems interact, and the organism constantly seeks to adjust to internal and external events to maintain homeostasis. The earth is envisioned as a giant biofeedback system, with any one part constantly influencing and being influenced by all the other parts. In this perspective, human beings are the consciousness of the organism and therefore bear the responsibility for intelligent use of the planet's resources to ensure its survival.

While not endorsing this organic view entirely, Pope John Paul II suggests a similar sense of interconnection in his 1988 encyclical *On Social Concern (Sollicitudo Rei Socialis)* when he writes: "One must take into account the nature of each being and of its mutual connection in an ordered system, which is precisely the 'cosmos.'"[4] While one might argue that the earth is not one biological organism, this view has the advantage of continually reminding us that all the dynamics of life on the planet are interconnected. There is at least a semi-organic unity that binds our destiny with the destiny of the ecological whole.

The *Catechism of the Catholic Church* speaks clearly of the interdependence of the created world:

> God wills *the interdependence of creatures.* The sun and the moon, the cedar and the little flower, the eagle and the sparrow: the

4. *On Social Concern* (Washington: United States Catholic Conference, 1988) no. 34.

spectacle of their countless diversities and inequalities tells us that no creature is self-sufficient. Creatures exist only in dependence on each other, to complete each other, in the service of each other.

The *beauty of the universe:* The order and harmony of the created world results from the diversity of beings and from the relationships which exist among them. Man discovers them progressively as the laws of nature. They call forth the admiration of scholars. The beauty of creation reflects the infinite beauty of the Creator and ought to inspire the respect and submission of man's intellect and will.[5]

Harmony and Health

Among the Native Americans, the Navajo (or the Dinee, in their language) perhaps best express a sense of the interconnections between the land and the well-being of humans. The Navajo approach to illness and healing revolves around a concept of *hozho,* which is the condition of beauty and harmony that existed at the beginning of creation. When the sacred order of creation is disturbed, illness results. The Navajo rituals for healing, then, aim to reconnect the patient with the proper order of things. When harmony is restored, health is restored. This harmony is expressed in the Navajo goal of "walking in beauty."

In modern Western medicine, too, there is a growing awareness of the links between physical and spiritual health and between the health of the environment and the health of human beings. We are increasingly aware of the impact of chemicals in the environment on human health, and we are gradually becoming more aware of the importance of a healthy environment for human well-being. Some suggest that the gradual depletion of the soil through the use of chemical fertilizers has affected the food supply to the point that our health is being jeopardized. Others believe that much of the cancer and other diseases that afflict contemporary society results from pollutants in the air and water. While much of this is still speculative, enough links have been found between

5. *Catechism of the Catholic Church* (Washington: United States Catholic Conference, 1994) nos. 340–341.

human health and cigarette smoke, toxic chemicals, lead in gasoline, paint, asbestos, radiation, etc., to make it clear that environmental problems have a definite effect on human health.

At the same time, we are becoming more and more conscious of the ways in which psychic and spiritual conditions affect the health of the human body. Much has been written about the effect of good mental health and/or a healthy spiritual outlook on recovery from illness and on prolonging both the quality and length of life, even among those with terminal conditions.

The Christian community has long recognized this holistic approach to sickness and health in its use of the sacrament of the anointing of the sick. In recent centuries this sacrament was reserved for those who were at death's door, but it has a longer history that expresses well the insight that physical and spiritual health are intimately linked. The celebration of the ritual for one who is sick encourages the patient to link his or her sufferings to those of Christ. This leads to a healing of spirit that may also result in a healing of the body. This sacrament also uses created material—the oil used in the anointing—along with human touch to mediate the divine presence. It thus reflects a sense of seeking harmony with God, humans, and all creation, a good example of the ecological awareness implicit in Christian worship.

Questions for Reflection and Discussion

1. How widespread do you think hyperindividualism is in American culture today? Do you see any signs of change in this, either positive or negative, in recent years? How much are you personally affected by this tendency to focus on self to the exclusion of communal concerns?

2. What can be done to increase concern for the common good? Is this an issue that must be handled primarily by the family, by the Church, by government, by the media? Where do we start?

3. Do you think humans in general have been more mindful of our dominance of creation or of our place within creation? How do we develop a stronger sense of our links with all elements of the environment? Can worship help develop this?

4. What environmental concerns can you name that require international action? How can we foster such global cooperation?

5. What images of the earth have helped you to see the necessity of global action? Can you remember when you first saw those images and how they affected you? Do you think of the whole earth as a living organism? Why or why not?

6. Does the Navajo (Dinee) perspective on healing and wholeness appeal to you? What is your own view of the relation between body and spirit in matters of sickness and health? Do you think that contemporary health problems are often related to environmental problems?

7. How do you understand the sacrament of the anointing of the sick today? Do you see it as a reflection of the Church's belief in the links between physical and spiritual healing?

Chapter Three

The Mystery of Incarnation

The little girl was afraid of the dark and had a hard time when she was put to bed. Time after time she came back to the family room, and mother had to take her back to bed. She begged her mother to stay with her all night. "I can't do that," her mother replied, "but you shouldn't be afraid because you are not alone. God is always with you." "But I don't want God," the little girl cried. "I want somebody with skin on!"

We who are Christians believe that we have a God "with skin on." A fundamental tenet of the Christian faith is summed up in the word "incarnation." This doctrine refers first of all to the enfleshment of the Son of God, who took on the human condition and became the God-Man, Jesus. He is God incarnate, God enfleshed. Jesus is the God-Man, fully divine and fully human at the same time. How this can be takes us into the realm of inexpressible mystery, but that it is so has been a foundation of our faith. The feast of the Incarnation (also called the Annunciation) celebrates his conception in the womb of the Virgin Mary, the beginning of our redemption in Christ.

From the earliest centuries, however, the Church has seen broader ramifications to this doctrine. If God is fully present in Jesus, then humanity and divinity have been inextricably linked. God may be encountered through human beings, not in some rarefied atmosphere of pure spirits. God has entered into creation so thoroughly that nothing is truly profane; everything is capable of revealing the presence of the sacred.

The writings of Pierre Teilhard de Chardin give contemporary expression to these implications of the Incarnation, but the insight is as old as Christianity itself. Martin Luther, the great sixteenth-century reformer, expressed it well: "Now if I believe in God's Son and bear in mind that he became man, *all* creatures will appear a hundred times more beautiful to me than before. Then I will properly appreciate the sun, the moon, the stars, trees, apples, and pears, and reflect that he is Lord over all and the center of all things."[1] Or as Teilhard put it, "By virtue of the Creation, and still more of the Incarnation, nothing here below is profane for those who know how to see."[2]

This perspective owes much to our ancestors in faith, the Jewish people, whose view of creation and of God's presence everywhere carries over into the Christian faith. The Jewish Scriptures frequently speak of creation praising God and revealing God's glory.

This linking of the human and the divine, of God and God's creation, has cast Christianity in a significantly different mode than other world religions. There is no real basis in Christianity for a rejection of the material world as evil, even though such spiritualities have arisen at various times in our history. The early Church, for example, resisted strongly the Gnostics and the Manicheans, who saw matter as evil and the spiritual life as a process of rising above matter. The Christian perspective sees creation as good, created by God and reflecting the beauty of God. It sees the material as capable of bearing the spiritual, reaching its high point in Jesus, who revealed the fullness of God in human form.

The Incarnation is the basis of the Christian sacramental system. The Church has followed Christ's example in using created things and human gestures as the means of encountering the divine. The experience of immersion in water or the pouring of water in baptism; the feel and aroma of the scented oil called chrism used at baptism, confirmation, and ordination; the touch of the human hand in penance and anointing of the sick and ordination; the taste of bread and wine in Eucharist; and the shared vows of love in marriage all express divine realities as well as powerful human experiences.

1. Quoted in *Bibelot*, vol. 4, nos. 4, 5, 6 (Dayton: United Theological Seminary, 1989) 6.

2. *The Divine Milieu* (New York: Collins and Harper & Row, 1960) 78.

Other created things also find their place in Christian worship: the incense that speaks of our prayer and of God's forgiveness; the wax of candles reminding us of Christ, the Light of the world; the wood of the cross as a sign of victory even more than a sign of suffering; statues and stained glass that call us to live in the communion of saints; the human voices that proclaim the word of God; the sounds of musical instruments and voices; and the processions and dances of members of the assembly. All these elements of worship give witness to the fundamental Christian belief in the Incarnation.

Christian worship generally takes place in buildings designed for and dedicated to that purpose. We commonly call them "churches," though they are more properly called the "houses of the Church," for the Church, the people of God, meets in them for worship. But the Christian perspective does not limit God's presence to the church building; rather, it sees God as present in all places and the whole of creation as God's sanctuary. Some have called this view a sense of the earth as enchanted. It recognizes that there is more to the earth than pure matter, that the spiritual is present in the material, and that the earth deserves our reverence.

As the German theologian Jürgen Moltmann put it, "the Creator, through his Spirit *dwells in* his creation as a whole, and in every individual created being, by virtue of his Spirit holding them together and keeping them in life. The inner secret of creation is this *indwelling of God. . . .*"[3] Pope Paul VI made a similar point in a speech to the Council of the World Wildlife Fund in 1969: "The image of the Creator must shine forth ever more clearly, not only in his creature Man, but in all of His creation in nature."[4] Father Thomas Berry insists that "the universe itself, but especially the planet Earth, needs to be experienced as the primary mode of the divine presence."[5]

---

3. *God in Creation: A New Theology of Creation and the Spirit of God* (Minneapolis: Fortress Press, 1993) xiv.

4. *Social Justice*, vol. 62 (Nov. 1969) 230.

5. *The Dream of the Earth* (San Francisco: Sierra Club Books, 1988) 120.

Pantheism vs. Respect for Creation

One of the dangers of venerating matter, a danger that has been recognized throughout Christian tradition, is the heresy of pantheism. This position states that God and creation are coterminous, that the universe is God and God is the universe. Fear of falling into this heresy has perhaps made many Christians hesitant in dealing with the created universe.

The Christian tradition insists on the transcendence of God, recognizing that God may be present within creation but cannot be reduced to creation. God transcends creation as an artist transcends his or her work. As the artist puts much of himself or herself in a painting but is not identified with the work, so the divine presence is found in the work of the divine Artist. Thus the Christian tradition also insists on the immanence of God: God can be found within all creation.

Without identifying God with creation, Christians must manifest a deep respect for creation. The eighth-century monk and theologian St. John Damascene wrote of venerating matter:

> I honor all matter and venerate it. Through it, filled, as it were, with a divine power and grace, my salvation has come to me. Was not the thrice happy and thrice blessed wood of the cross matter? Was not the sacred and holy mountain of Calvary matter? What of the life-giving rock, the holy sepulchre, the Source of our resurrection: was it not matter? Is not the most holy book of the gospels matter? Is not the blessed table matter which gives us the bread of life? Are not the gold and silver matter, out of which crosses and altarplate and chalices are made? And before all these things, is not the body and blood of our Lord matter? . . . Do not despise matter, for it is not despicable.[6]

Such language can remind us that Christianity is really the most materialistic of all religions. Preachers often rail against the materialism of our age. Properly understood, most Christians need to be more materialistic rather than less. The problem is that we often misuse the material world, but the solution is not to avoid

6. "Holy Images" 16, *Word and Redeemer: Christology in the Fathers,* ed. James M. Carmody, S.J., and Thomas E. Clarke, S.J. (Glen Rock, N.J.: Paulist Press, 1966) 120.

matter but to use it according to God's will. And that begins with a profound respect for all parts of creation as God's work.

This attitude of respect for creation is a necessary balance to the sense of dominion over creation so often attributed to the book of Genesis. Human beings are placed over creation, but such dominion does not mean domination and destruction. As Pope Paul VI said in a speech to the United Nations Food and Agriculture Organization in 1970:

> It took millennia for man to learn to dominate, "to subdue the earth," according to the inspired word of the first book of the Bible. The hour has now come for him to dominate his domination; this essential undertaking requires no less courage and dauntlessness than the conquest of nature itself.[7]

Fear of Embodied Worship

Probably the most difficult consequence of the Incarnation for many Christians to embrace is its implication that the human body is also sacred and a primary mode of God's revelation. Because physical desires are so strong and so easily misused, Christians have always been tempted to see the body as evil. Seeing the body as evil quickly leads to seeing all physical reality as evil. The material is seen as opposed to the spiritual.

Our bodies are an integral part of creation, and our links to the rest of the created world are most obvious when we consider our bodies. We need food and drink to sustain our life. We need plants and animals to provide both food and clothing. We need trees and mineral resources to build homes and furniture and automobiles and machinery. We need air to breathe and water for drinking and bathing. We need a thousand and one elements of creation because our bodies are material and are intricately linked with the whole material world.

It is crucial, then, if we are ever to achieve a holistic view of creation, to come to terms with our fears and doubts about the sacredness of our bodies. In the early third century, the

7. *The Teachings of Pope Paul VI, 1970* (Washington: United States Catholic Conference, 1971) 398.

North African theologian Tertullian called the flesh the "pivot" of salvation:

> To such a degree is the flesh the pivot of salvation, that since by it the soul becomes linked with God, it is the flesh which makes possible the soul's election by God. For example, the flesh is washed that the soul may be made spotless: the flesh is anointed that the soul may be consecrated: the flesh is signed (with the cross) that the soul too may be protected: the flesh is overshadowed by the imposition of the hand that the soul may be illumined by the Spirit: the flesh feeds on the Body and Blood of Christ that the soul also may be replete with God.[8]

Our problems with our bodies often are most manifest when it comes to worship. Since Christian worship is incarnational, it presumes a certain level of comfort with the body. The sacraments are all physical in various ways. Baptism by immersion, long the standard mode of baptizing, is again the preferred mode in the Catholic Church. Such an experience, whether done in the nude as in ancient times or in swimming apparel or robes, is clearly an involving bodily experience. Before baptism, catechumens are signed on the forehead, on the eyes, on the ears, on the lips, over the heart, on the shoulders, on the hands, and on the feet, signifying the dedication of the whole body to Christ. After baptism, initiates are anointed with perfumed oil for confirmation; in ancient times the oil was put over the whole body, but today only the head is anointed. In the Eucharist we share bread and wine, two basic foods to sustain body and spirit. In reconciliation, in ordination, and in the anointing of the sick, hands are imposed as a sign of the Spirit's presence. Oddly enough, the sacrament that has the least physical ritual is that of marriage, but the whole sacrament presumes the potential of the body and of physical love to mediate the presence of Christ to the couple.

In addition to these basic sacramental ritual symbols, Christian worship embraces the body in numerous ways. We bless our bodies with water when we enter church as a reminder of baptism, and water is sometimes sprinkled on us

8. *Tertullian's Treatise on the Resurrection,* ch. 8, trans. Ernest Evans (London: SPCK, 1960) 25.

more fully for the same purpose. We sit and stand and kneel to express our attention and our reverence. Our bodies are incensed, both in life on various occasions and after death during the Mass of Christian burial. We bow and genuflect, we process and dance, we exchange the sign of peace, we join hands in unity and raise hands in praise. In short, we use our bodies in almost every imaginable way to give praise to God, and we honor our bodies as temples of the Holy Spirit and members of the body of Christ.

It is no secret that dealing with the body remains a difficult issue for many Christians. While we recognize that the body, like any gift of God, can be misused for sin, we need also to accept more fully that it is a gift of God and sacred in God's sight. We need to learn more deeply that our bodies are temples of the Spirit and that, through the Spirit, Christ dwells in our bodies. The more we come to terms with our bodily nature, the more likely we will be to embrace all creation as sacred, as the means by which God can reveal the divine presence. This growth in awareness will be a boon both to the ecological movement and to Christian worship.

Embodying the Divine in Our Lives

Coming to terms with our bodies in worship should also help us learn to deal with our bodies in a healthier way outside worship. Our culture both glorifies and demeans the body. Our confusion about sexuality prompts us on one hand to extol sex as the ultimate experience and the meaning of life, while on the other hand we continue to experience shame and embarrassment about our bodies and our sexuality. We also abuse our bodies frequently by overeating, by alcohol, drugs, and cigarettes, and by promiscuity. We do not cherish our bodies as temples of the Lord.

If we could learn to reverence our bodies as the liturgy does, then we might be able to enjoy bodily pleasures, including sex, without overindulging or misusing such joys. We might be able to avoid the extremes of overvaluing or rejecting our bodies. And we might be able to see our bodies as instruments for making God present in the world. Through baptism we have become members of the body of Christ. Christ is present in the world today through us. Just as we need to learn to see the face of Christ in those we meet, we are called to let Christ be enfleshed in our bodies today. A hymn attributed to St. Patrick says it well: "Christ be the vision in eyes that see me, in ears that hear me, Christ ever be."

Properly valuing our bodies can also help us live in harmony with all of creation. As we cherish our bodies, we come to cherish the material creation of which they are a part.

Questions for Reflection and Discussion

1. How central is the Incarnation in your personal faith perspective? How much does this doctrine influence your view of all creation?

2. Can you recall an occasion when you experienced powerfully the presence of God in creation? How would you describe or explain the experience?

3. Do the sacraments help you to be more fully in touch with God's creation? Have you recognized how central sacramental worship is to the Christian (and especially Catholic) tradition? Do the sacraments help you become more aware of God's presence in the created and the human?

4. Is pantheism a danger today? How do we avoid a pantheistic view and still develop a profound respect for creation as a means of encountering God?

5. How comfortable are you with your body at worship? Would a healthier perspective on our bodies help Christians to reverence themselves and all creation more deeply?

6. Can you see increased emphasis on bodily involvement in the renewal of worship since the Second Vatican Council? Do the sacraments help you to value your body as a temple of God?

7. How can you better embody God's presence in your own life? Would this have any effect on your dealings with other people and with the environment?

Chapter Four

Cultivating a Sense of Awe and Wonder

One of the wonders of the varied landscapes of North America is now a national park in Utah known as Bryce Canyon. The combination of wind and water has eroded the soft stone of the area in amazing ways, leaving columns and spires and "windows" of rock, all colored in a riot of hues by various mineral contents. The area is a maze of deep-cut chasms and canyons. It is at once an eerie and awesome sight, unlike any other spot on earth. An old rancher, seeing the sight for the first time, was heard to remark: "That's a heck of a place to lose a cow in!" Wonder and awe are not always the first reaction we humans have to the world around us!

Humility and Praise vs. Arrogance

A fundamental basis for worship is a sense of awe and wonder. It is the basic emotion that leads one instinctively to praise and thanksgiving, which form the heart of Christian worship. A sense of awe is closely linked to the virtue of humility. Barbara Budde quotes a member of the Iroquois nation she heard on PBS as follows: "Our ceremonies are in thanksgiving and appreciation for these life essences: corn, beans, the sun and rain. The industrial countries don't have ceremonies, they have pomp and circumstance. What we do takes humility, not pomp."[1]

1. "The Future of Festivity," *Assembly*, vol. 18, no. 2 (March 1992) 555.

Humility is the opposite of the arrogance that leads to environmental destruction. Humility involves the recognition that God is Lord and we are servants, not masters. This is a fundamental position of those who worship, for worship implies a God who deserves our praise and our thanks. This may be the most fundamental contribution of Christian worship to the ecological crisis: the recognition that God exists and is the master of the universe.

It is precisely the rejection of God as the source of creation and the master of the universe that leads to the greatest environmental disasters. When humans begin to think of themselves as sitting in the driver's seat of the universe, they wreak havoc in every direction. Only when we acknowledge our subordinate position, recognizing that the universe belongs to the Lord and that we are only stewards, will we learn to treat all creation according to God's will. And God's will for creation is embedded in its very structure and essence. Since all creation is interrelated and interdependent, it is clear that God intended all creation to live in harmony.

The exact lines of that harmony may be less clear than we would wish. Nature is full of violence and destruction. Some species survive only by the death of other species, and human beings are perhaps the most obviously dependent on other parts of creation for survival. Yet seeking to live in harmony with creation is still possible and necessary. The Native American peoples offer an example of humans living in harmony even while killing animals for food and clothing and shelter. The relationship of the Plains Indians with the American bison manifested a great reverence for the animals on which their lives depended. Before the hunt, it was common to ask the forgiveness of the bison and to honor it for giving its life to sustain the tribe. We may not adopt the forms of Native American rituals, but we need to adopt their basic sense of living in harmony with their environment.

The Awesomeness of Nature

The environment itself can help us develop a heightened sense of awe and wonder if we but pay attention. Standing beneath a giant sequoia is a quick lesson in humility. Those giant trees, the largest living things on the planet, tower over two hundred feet into the air and grow to over thirty feet in diameter at the base. They live for over three thousand years, which means that some of them were at their mature height before the birth of Christ. It is possible, of course, to look upon such a wonder as just a massive source of siding or shingles, but it is hard not to be awed by such majesty.

In a similar way, the splendor of the mountains and the rush of waterfalls in the American Rockies or the European Alps or the Asian Himalayas easily lead human beings to a sense of awe and wonder and then to praise of the Creator who fashioned them. Equally impressive are sights like the Great Plains, the vast deserts, the Grand Canyon, and the oceans of the world. Undersea exploration and travel to distant planets continue to fascinate humanity and should also lead us to wonder and praise.

The Immense and the Microscopic

The vastness of the universe itself naturally puts humans in a more humble light; it is hard to be puffed up with self-importance in the face of such enormity. To realize that light is just now reaching the earth from stars that burned out thousands of years ago reminds us of how short the whole history of the human race is in the context of the age of the universe. The distances and eons that are revealed in our investigations of the universe are beyond human comprehension. On the other hand, we have not yet discovered any other planet capable of sustaining life as we know it. This can remind us of how special we are to the Creator of all and also of how crucial it is that we preserve the spaceship earth on which we live.

When we turn the telescope around and look through a microscope, we are again led to wonder and awe. The complexity and vastness of the very smallest parts of creation are also capable of engendering humility. The number of living things in a single drop of pond water is overwhelming. Miracles of life abound all around us, too often unnoticed and uncelebrated.

The poet Marcia Hans raises the question this way: "Fueled by a million man-made wings of fire, the rocket tore a tunnel through the sky and everybody cheered. Fueled only by a thought from God, the seedling urged its way through the thickness of black, and as it pierced the heavy-ceiling of the soil and launched itself up into other space, no one even clapped."[2] It is so easy to overlook the manifold small wonders that mark every day. Spending time contemplating the small miracles that surround us would also lead us to humility and to praise.

Contemplation vs. Utilitarianism

Much of the misuse of creation can be attributed to an attitude that approaches things purely in light of their utility. Things have no value in themselves but are valuable only to the extent that they serve the needs or desires of human beings. The contrasting approach to creation is called contemplation. This word is often misunderstood as something reserved to monastics or hermits who spend all their time in contemplative prayer. Contemplation simply means to see things as they are in themselves, to look lovingly on a person or a thing, and to appreciate its inherent beauty.

The United States Department of Agriculture receives many requests for help from nonfarmers who have problems with gardens or lawns. One citizen wrote asking assistance with dandelions. He really loved his lawn, he wrote, but it was in danger of becoming overrun with dandelions. Some wise employee of the Agriculture Department wrote back and suggested that he learn to love dandelions, too.

The ultimate form of contemplation, of course, is to contemplate God, but a contemplative lifestyle also seeks to see all things with the same kind of loving and attentive gaze. To sit and marvel at the infinite variety of sounds made by a gurgling brook is contemplation. To stand in awe before the majesty of a giant sequoia is contemplation. To see, really see, the marvelous beauty of a flower, even a dandelion, is contemplation.

2. Quoted by Norm White in "Why, When a Seed Stirs, Does Nobody Clap?" *National Catholic Reporter* (July 13, 1990) 2.

To be a contemplative is to see each part of creation as a wonder in itself, to cheer when a seed sprouts, to clap in appreciation as the sun sets, to cherish the song of the chickadee, to rejoice in the freshness of a spring morning, to marvel at the grandeur of a mountain, to wonder at the colors of a rainbow.

Contemplation shapes our response to human creativity, too. To be contemplative is to rejoice in the music of Mozart, to marvel at the sculpture of Michelangelo, to be amazed by the power of a computer chip, to appreciate the complexity of a space mission, to rejoice in the soaring spaces enclosed by great architecture, to cherish the words of the poet, to be grateful for the countless inventions that enrich our lives.

Contemplation also notices the small things of life. To be contemplative is to marvel at how yeast makes bread rise, to rejoice at how grape juice becomes wine, to cherish the gentle touch of a loved one, to appreciate the soothing warmth of an ointment, to ponder the words of a friend, to welcome the embrace of a lover, to celebrate life in song and in silence. To be contemplative is to try to see the world as God sees it, in all its wonder and mystery. The contemplative seeks to be and to grow more than to have and to consume.

The liturgy teaches us to be contemplatives. It lifts up various parts of creation and helps us to see that they are capable of bearing the weight of divine majesty. Water and oil, bread and wine, words and gestures, men and women—all are marvelous mysteries in themselves and also capable of putting us in touch with the mystery of the divine presence at the heart of all creation.

Too often we have tried to seek God by separating ourselves from creation and even from our own bodies, by trying to become "purely spiritual." The message of the Incarnation is that God has chosen to come to us, not in spite of created things and other people, but precisely through creation and others. The contemplative gaze does not seek God outside the world but at its heart. The contemplative person does not seek to ignore creation but to look more deeply into it and find the divine presence there. As Teilhard de Chardin put it, "Let us leave the surface and, without leaving the world, plunge into God."

It must be admitted that our worship experience may not always measure up to this kind of contemplative stance. As a people geared to production and results, we often approach worship in a similar fashion, looking for tangible results and asking what worship accomplishes. But a proper approach to worship recognizes the importance of simply being in God's presence, experiencing God's loving care, giving thanks for the gifts of God, and spending time together with other Christians as the body of Christ.

Such contemplation of God in the midst of creation is the core meaning of worship. Liturgy does affect us in various beneficial ways, but the Christian commitment to worship is not oriented to producing such effects. They are simply wonderful side effects of taking time to contemplate the wonder of God's love revealed in creation and in the redemptive work of Jesus Christ.

A Contemplative Approach to the Environment

A more contemplative stance toward the natural world would be of great benefit in preserving the environment. We need to learn to cherish all that is simply because it is, to appreciate the beauty of every part of creation, whether or not it is "useful" to human beings. Such respect for creation would make us less likely to destroy or damage the environment.

Contemplation can also help us to keep perspective in our relationship to creation. John Muir used to ridicule the very idea of humans "conquering" a mountain by reaching its peak. "When a mountain is climbed it is said to be conquered—as well say a man is conquered when a fly lights on his head."[3] The mountain invites our contemplation, not our domination. We are stewards of creation, not its masters. We need to respect and cherish every part of creation rather than seeking to dominate it as if we owned it.

3. *John Muir Summering in the Sierra* (Madison, Wis.: Univ. of Wisconsin Press, 1984) 149.

Worship in the Woods

Many people have explained their absence from Christian worship on Sunday by insisting that they can worship better in the woods than in church. Of course, many of them don't worship in the woods each Sunday either, but the point is still worth consideration. We need Christian worship for its fellowship and community. We are members of Christ's body, so we need to worship together. But it remains true that many people can sense the presence of the Lord more easily in the midst of nature than in the midst of the worshiping assembly. While this might lead us to some healthy questioning about the state of our worship and our worship spaces, it may also be that even the best worship experience in the best worship space possible will never be as powerful for some people as the experience of God in nature.

This fact should not induce us to posit an opposition between finding God in nature and encountering the Lord in worship. The two experiences should be complementary rather than conflicting. To be aware of God in nature should lead us to praise the Lord with the Christian assembly in worship. And our experience of worship should make us more aware of God in all of creation. The relationship between ecology and worship is truly of mutual benefit.

The Religious Experience

The religious experience, properly understood, provides the best foundation for a lasting ecological awareness. Richard Austin, a biographer of the naturalist John Muir, makes the point well: "Knowledge alone will not protect nature, nor will ethics, for by themselves they do not arouse motivation strong enough to transform the exploitative patterns to which we have become accustomed. The protection of nature must be rooted in love and delight—in religious experience."[4] Far too often, those who espouse a greater ecological sensitivity find the struggle too hard and the quest too long to endure. It is all

4. *Baptized into Wilderness: A Christian Perspective on John Muir* (Atlanta: John Knox Press, 1987) 3.

too common for people to get enthused about recycling and fighting pollution and stopping the cutting of the rain forests, but then to lose interest when things seem to change so little and the effort becomes difficult. The religious experience provides the lasting motivation to continue the effort because it finds God, the source of all meaning, in the midst of creation. The reverence we owe to God is linked to the reverence we show to the Creator's work.

A Sense of Thanksgiving

To the extent that we acquire a sense of wonder and awe at creation, we are naturally moved to give thanks to the One who created it all. An attitude of gratitude leads one to a more respectful response to creation. Just as we cherish any gift given to us by one who loves us, so we come to cherish creation as a gift. As we recognize that destroying a gift from another expresses ungratefulness, so we recognize that destroying creation is ungrateful to the Creator.

Charles Dickens once told an audience that he felt we Americans had it backwards when it came to Thanksgiving Day. He suggested that we should have one day a year for griping and complaining and then use the other 364 days to thank God for the many blessings we have received.

Christian worship is fundamentally a response of thanksgiving. Worship is a response to what God has done and continues to do for us. The very term "eucharist," the primary Christian form of worship, means "thanksgiving." The liturgy constantly leads us to offer thanks and praise to God for the gifts of creation and redemption. Participating regularly in this liturgy ought to gradually teach us to live constantly with a sense of profound gratitude. Each day of our lives should be a thanksgiving day. If we acquire such a viewpoint, we are much more likely to care for creation as God's gift and thus to avoid abuse of the environment.

Questions for Reflection and Discussion

1. Can you recall an experience that left you speechless with awe and wonder? What made it so powerful for you?

2. Does your experience of worship help you grow in humility? Can you imagine how a life devoid of worship might create a very different perspective on the proper role of human beings in the world?

3. Does your experience of nature prompt a sense of humility? What experiences in particular can you recall that put humanity in perspective for you?

4. What is the most significant point about the vastness of the universe to you? What is the most marvelous small wonder you have experienced?

5. Do you think of yourself as a contemplative? How would you develop a more contemplative approach to life? Does the liturgy help you move in this direction?

6. Do you find it easy to pray in the midst of nature? How does this relate to your experience of worship in church?

7. Does the liturgy and your prayer life support you in environmental work? How do you cope with the difficulty of dealing with such vast problems?

8. How much is gratitude a theme of your life? Do you find that the liturgy is an expression of your own gratitude? What might make you more aware of how much God has gifted your life?

9. Does Thanksgiving Day remind you to treat creation with respect and gratitude? How could this be extended to every day of the year? Do meal prayers help you to recognize the goodness of creation as God's gift?

Chapter Five

Private Property vs. Common Good

The story is told of a Chinese rice farmer whose land was near the temple on a hilltop overlooking the coastal land of his neighbors. An earthquake struck and everyone ran out into the fields. From his position on the hill, this farmer could see that the sea had withdrawn from the shore and was being gathered up into a tidal wave. He was too far away to be heard if he tried yelling to warn his neighbors, so without hesitation he quickly set fire to his own rice and began ringing the temple bell. His neighbors, seeing the smoke, quickly came to his aid. His crop was a total loss, but when the tidal wave hit, all the neighbors were on the hill and their lives were saved. The farmer had recognized his obligation to the community as more important than his own property.

The approach that people take to creation is often revealed in their attitude toward private property. Our culture has put great value on the individual's right to own property with little or no restriction. Efforts to limit environmental damage often come into conflict with the perceived rights of individuals to use their property as they see fit. Polluters argue that they should be able to do what they want to the land they own. Agribusiness depletes the soil for short-term profit without regard for future needs. Those who burn the rain forests say that their actions are not the business of anyone in other countries. Businesses fight air pollution controls because they limit profits. And countless individual consumers swell the garbage stream with material that could be recycled, but they insist that nobody can tell them they have to sort their trash.

The "Social Mortgage" on Private Property

The Catholic Church has long upheld the right of private property, but it does not see that right as absolute. Pope John Paul II has spoken of the limits on private ownership as a "social mortgage." Those who own property have a duty to serve the common good of all. There is an inevitable tension between the common good and private property rights, but a healthy tension must be maintained. The individual must not be completely subordinated to the will of the community, but neither must the needs of the community be completely subordinated to the desire for personal profit and individual freedom.

The Catholic bishops of the United States expressed a similar perspective in their pastoral letter on the economy in 1986, insisting that "freedom of entrepreneurship, business and finance should be protected, but the accountability of this freedom to the common good and the norms of justice must be assured." They added that "no one can ever own capital resources absolutely or control their use without regard for others and society as a whole. This applies first of all to land and natural resources."[1]

This perspective is not a common one in our society, but we do seem to be gradually learning that there must be limits on the right of private property for the sake of the common good. The growth in environmental legislation is one sign of that recognition. Another is the increasing recognition among executives of corporations that they must take social and community concerns into account in their business decisions. There is much more that must be developed in this area, but there are signs of hope.

---

1. *Economic Justice for All: Pastoral Letter on Catholic Social Teaching and the U.S. Economy* (Washington: National Conference of Catholic Bishops, 1986) nos. 110, 112.

Stewardship vs. Ownership

The limits on the right to private property required by the common good are paralleled by the limits on human dominion over the rest of creation. Human beings do not have absolute dominion; we are stewards more than owners. In his encyclical *On Social Concern (Sollicitudo Rei Socialis)*, Pope John Paul II insists that

> the dominion granted to man by the Creator is not an absolute power, nor can one speak of a freedom to "use and misuse" or to dispose of things as one pleases. The limitation imposed from the beginning by the Creator himself and expressed symbolically by the prohibition not to "eat of the fruit of the tree" (cf. Gen. 2:16-17) shows clearly enough that, when it comes to the natural world, we are subject not only to biological laws but also to moral ones, which cannot be violated with impunity."[2]

This perspective on property rights flows from the basic biblical perspective that the earth belongs to the Lord.

> The Lord's are the earth and its fullness,
>   the world and those who dwell in it.
> For he founded it upon the seas
>   and established it upon the rivers (Ps. 24:1-2).

The earth has been given to us for our use, but it does not ultimately belong to us; we are stewards charged with the proper care and maintenance of the earth. Even those who do not base their position on faith in God can recognize that the earth does not really belong to us. As many have noted, in destroying our environment we are squandering our children's inheritance. Each generation occupies the earth for a short time, and during that time we have the use of the earth's resources. But we also have the obligation to preserve those resources for future generations and not to squander them with selfish greed. Those who do believe in God have even more reason to be good stewards of all that has been entrusted to us.

From a faith perspective, we believe that the earth is given by God for the good of all people, both those presently on the

2. *On Social Concern* (Washington: United States Catholic Conference, 1988) no. 34.

earth and those yet to come. St. Ambrose, writing in Milan in the fourth century, put it well: "Nature has poured forth all things in common for all. For God has commanded that all things be brought forth so that there might be food for all in common and that the earth may be the common possession of all. Nature, therefore, has produced a common right, but greed has made it into a private right."[3]

This view of creation as belonging to all people has radical implications for questions of justice when a small percentage of the world's population in the developed countries consumes the majority of the earth's resources. Recent popes have repeatedly called for a new economic order that would do a better job of sharing the resources of the earth with all the people of the earth.

The earth has been entrusted to us as its caretakers. Unfortunately, we humans have too often acted as leavetakers rather than caretakers. As the letter from Chief Seattle noted (see pp. 3–4), we come to a section of the earth, use its resources with no regard for the future, and then leave the land barren and destroyed while we go off to find new land to plunder.

The increasing world population and lack of new land to claim is beginning to reveal the folly of this approach, but it still reigns among those who place short-term profit ahead of all other concerns. Often the land and its resources are still being plundered with little regard for future needs. Sustainable agriculture and lumbering, mining practices that preserve the land, conservation of natural resources, recycling, and other preservation efforts must become the normal way of life among all people and nations if the planet is to survive and sustain future generations.

Worship and the Collection

The experience of worship offers a strong reminder of our true status in the universe. We recognize God's sovereignty over all creation every time we gather to worship the Lord. We acknowledge our position as recipients of God's gifts and

3. "On the Duties of the Clergy," bk. 1, ch. 28, par. 132; PL 16:62.

admit our failings to use those gifts rightly. We respond to God's generosity by offering praise and thanksgiving for all God has given us. All these attitudes support an awareness that we are not the masters of the universe, not the absolute owners of creation.

A particular moment in Sunday worship that is found in almost every denomination has special relevance to this point. Every Sunday the assembly is asked to contribute to the collection for the needs of the poor and the Church. This obligation is often seen as simply a burden imposed by the need to maintain the church building and parish programs and occasionally to respond to the pleas of the needy. But its significance as part of the liturgy is much deeper.

The collection of money is a symbolic as well as a practical act. When we give a portion of our income to God, we are admitting that we have a responsibility beyond our own self-preservation. We give back to God, first of all, because God has given to us. The collection is a symbol of gratitude and a reminder that all we have is gift from God.

In a deeper sense, the collection should remind us that the gifts we have received do not ultimately belong to us; they are given to us for our use, but all that we have really belongs to God. We give a portion of it back to remind ourselves that all of it must be used according to God's will and to foster God's kingdom. Just as the offering of the firstfruits of the harvest in the Jewish tradition symbolized the whole harvest, so our monetary offering symbolizes all that God gives us. We give it back to God, which is to say we commit ourselves to using all of it according to God's will.

A small church was celebrating the anniversary of its founding, and former members were invited to share in the service. One of them had become a millionaire, and during the gathering he recounted a story from his youth. He had earned his first dollar and had decided to keep it forever. But then a visiting missionary had spoken at the church about the great needs of the missions, and after much debate with himself, he gave the dollar to the missions. "I am convinced," he said, "that God blessed me so richly because I gave God all I possessed when I was a boy." With that, an elderly man in the congregation stood and said to him, "Brother, I dare you to do it again!"

Such is the ultimate meaning of the collection. We may not actually give everything we possess, but what we give represents the whole. Whatever is given should be given to God, whether it goes for the work of the Church or directly to the needs of the poor. The judgment scene in Matthew 25 makes it abundantly clear that we give to Christ by giving food to the hungry, drink to the thirsty, clothing to the naked, shelter to the homeless, and comfort to the sick and imprisoned. Various Christian writers through the centuries have insisted that when we keep more of the world's goods than we really need, we are stealing from the poor.

Our experience of worship as a whole and the collection in particular should serve to remind us continually that we are stewards of God's gifts and that they must be used for the good of all.

Questions for Reflection and Discussion

1. Do you own property? How do you view it? Do you feel that you own more or less than your share of the earth's land and goods?

2. What does the term "social mortgage" mean to you? Does the Holy Father's view of private property make sense to you? How do you think most people in our culture respond to such ideas?

3. What is the difference between stewardship and ownership? What practical difference might this distinction have on the way we treat what we "own"?

4. Can you think of areas of the earth that humans have destroyed and then deserted? Is the process continuing today? How do we change that pattern?

5. What does the collection at the Eucharist mean to you? Is it just a practical necessity or does it have symbolic value? What could be done to make its symbolic meaning more evident?

Chapter Six

Social Justice and the Environment

Before Abraham Lincoln became president, he was walking down the street one day in Springfield, Illinois, with two of his sons. Both boys were crying loudly, and a passerby asked Lincoln what was the matter with the boys. "Just what's the matter with the whole world," Lincoln said. "I've got three walnuts, and each wants two."

Those who work to preserve the environment frequently find themselves immersed in issues of social justice. Much of the devastation that occurs around the world is intimately linked to conditions of injustice. Sometimes the environmental destruction results in unjust conditions for inhabitants of an area. The rape of the Appalachian mountain region by mining interests has destroyed much of the land, polluted the streams, and left widespread poverty affecting millions. The wreck of the Exxon Valdez not only destroyed the pristine beauty of Prince William Sound and killed vast numbers of animals and fish, but its aftermath also affected the livelihood of numerous fisherman and others in the region. The Chernobyl disaster resulted in disease and death for countless numbers of people and deprived many survivors of their homes and property. Unrestrained logging in Haiti has left a devastated and poverty-stricken country with eroded slopes in place of beautiful mountains. Similar devastation in the Philippines has caused widespread erosion and the destruction of the livelihood of fishermen as the soil runs off and ruins the feeding and spawning grounds of fish.

The issues are often linked in the other direction as well. When people are reduced to such poverty that survival is in question, the environment is often degraded as people seek to eke out an existence. The need for wood for cooking and heating can lead to overcutting of trees. The lack of resources for proper sanitation and sewage results in pollution of the land and the water. The need to raise every possible bit of food leads to depletion and erosion of the soil. The quest for land to grow crops leads to the cutting of the rain forests. Environmental degradation leads to poverty, and poverty leads to further environmental degradation.

War and Peace

As recent history makes clear, the poverty that leads to such devastation of the environment is often a result of oppression and war. Many of the famines in Africa in recent decades have resulted more from the destruction and dislocations caused by war than from natural disasters such as droughts. Starvation is used as a weapon, crops are destroyed in enemy territories, and relief supplies are prevented from reaching the population. Such crimes cry out to heaven for redress, and they frequently result in radical destruction of the ecology of the regions involved.

Even when widespread poverty is not the result, war is a major cause of environmental disasters. Chemicals are used to destroy people and animals, or defoliants are used to destroy vegetation. The land is contaminated, either on purpose or as a side effect of bombs and artillery. During the Gulf War, Iraq set oil wells ablaze all over Kuwait with widespread ecological consequences.

Even beyond the direct effects of war, the amount of money and resources given over to war and war preparations has a drastic effect on the distribution of the world's goods, leading to poverty and the environmental destruction it fosters. President Dwight D. Eisenhower, a five-star general and war hero of World War II, noted this dynamic: "Every gun that is made, every warship launched, every rocket fired, signifies, in the final sense, a theft from those who hunger and are not fed, those who are cold and are not clothed."[1] The magnitude of the military budgets of both sides in the cold war for the past four decades has wrought untold suffering upon the poor of the world. And the more people are forced to live in poverty, the greater the destruction of the natural environment that results. Learning to live in peace may be the greatest step the human race could take to preserve the environment of the planet.

Peace and the Liturgy

Though war has been a constant fact of human history, participation in the liturgy calls us to peace. The reforms of the Second Vatican Council restored the ritual sign of peace as part of the Eucharistic liturgy. This simple ritual stands as a strong symbol of the unity we are called to share in Christ. While it clearly does not produce world peace by itself, peace grows in the world person by person. As we tear down the walls that divide people from one another, we gradually learn to live in peace with one another. The difficulty many Catholics had with the restoration of the sign of peace indicates how easy it is to become isolated from others and the necessity of constantly reaching out. The sign of peace is not the only facet of worship that urges us to live in peace, but it has made the issue clear to many people.

In the Roman tradition, the sign of peace has been part of the communion rite, an integral part of our immediate preparation for joining in communion with one another in Christ. The act of communion itself is the strongest motive for living in peace, for we share the same body and blood of the Lord and are bound closely to one another. Unfortunately, many Christians seem blithely unaware that communion with the Lord also means communion with all members of his body. Here again, the awareness that the assembly has of the pres-

1. "The Chance for Peace," address to the American Society of Newspaper Editors, April 16, 1953, in *The Public Papers of the Presidents of the United States: Dwight Eisenhower* (Washington: Office of the Federal Register, 1953) 182.

ence of Christ in one another can contribute greatly to the full experience of the Eucharist.

Acts of repentance and reconciliation in worship, whether in the sacrament of reconciliation or in the Eucharist or in other rituals, can also help to form us as people of peace. Human interaction in day-to-day life always produces conflict and hurts. Whether the conflict is between people, groups, or nations, there are ultimately only two ways to respond: to seek revenge or to forgive. To seek revenge is the way to war; to learn to forgive is the way to peace. The ritual experience of reconciliation in worship ought to make us quicker to forgive in every area of our lives and less apt to respond belligerently. If we learn to forgive on a person-to-person basis, we might eventually learn how to respond to international conflicts in peaceful ways as well.

The potential of worship to shape us as a people of peace has not been fully exploited in times past. The Catholic bishops of the United States, in their pastoral letter on war and peace in 1983, called for more attention to the power of the Eucharist in particular to express and sustain our commitment to working for peace.[2] The very experience of Eucharist itself, even without the sign of peace, always calls us to unity with Christ and with his gift of himself for the salvation of the whole world. Our sharing in communion unites us with all the members of the body of Christ, a worldwide communion that ought to be constantly working to preserve peace among all peoples.

Poverty vs. Sharing

Working to preserve the environment requires working to overcome the conditions of poverty that afflict so many around the world. Only when people have the basics necessary to sustain life can we realistically expect them to take steps to preserve the environment for future generations. The disparity of wealth between rich and poor nations as well as within nations is a significant cause of environmental degradation, as we noted earlier.

2. See *The Challenge of Peace: God's Promise and Our Response* (Washington: United States Catholic Conference, 1983) no. 295.

To live on this planet in a sustainable fashion will require a different attitude toward life and the accumulation of wealth. The fall of the communist regimes in most of the world has discredited socialism and led many to conclude that Western capitalism is the clear victor and the only way to structure an economic system. While it may be true that self-interest and the profit motive, which underlie capitalism, are the best ways to motivate people to foster economic growth, it is also true that unrestrained capitalism causes widespread inequity and significant environmental damage. What is needed is an attitude that looks at the world's resources and wealth as gifts to be shared rather than private property to be accumulated as extravagantly as possible. The selfish impulse that capitalism nurtures must be balanced by a strong sense, not only of charity toward the needy, but of a justice that recognizes the basic rights of all people to the necessities of life.

The Eucharist fosters the attitude that we need here. There is great ritual significance in the fact that in the Eucharistic meal all share the same food and drink equally. No one receives a greater portion because of greater wealth or status or power. Those distinguishing characteristics have no currency in the midst of worship. Here we are all equal, all sons and daughters of God, brothers and sisters of Christ, one family in the Lord. And we share in the same body and blood of Christ equally.

In his first letter to the Corinthians (11:17-34), St. Paul chastised the early Christian community because they had violated this basic principle at the Eucharistic meal. The rich were eating sumptuously while the poor had little. It may well be that the separation of the ritual communion from the community meal resulted from this inequity. It was simply not acceptable to express the divisions caused by wealth and poverty in the context of worship.

The Eucharistic sharing in communion calls us to a sharing of goods beyond the Eucharist as well. To continue to celebrate Eucharist without seeking ways to redress the wide inequality in the use of the world's goods that pervades our world is to engage in a worship that is not authentic or honest.

Simplicity of Life vs. Consumerism

The story is told of a man who moved into an Amish community, bringing with him a new refrigerator with a built-in icemaker, a deluxe stereo system with a CD player, a color television and a VCR, a new computer, portable phones, and other similar high-tech items. The day after he moved in, his Amish neighbors came to call, bringing some homemade bread as a welcoming gift. As they left, the Amish man volunteered his help if anything went wrong with any of that array of equipment. "Thank you very much," said the new arrival. "No problem," the Amish man replied, "I'll just tell you how to get along without them!"

Coming to terms with the demands of justice in sharing the world's resources eventually forces us to ask questions about the lifestyle of the majority of people in the developed countries. Our own country alone consumes a vastly disproportionate share of the world's resources. While we may be able to continue economic growth worldwide and thus help to alleviate the suffering and deprivation of the world's poor, it is rather obvious that we cannot continue to maintain the degree of disparity that has long existed between the developed industrialized nations and the rest of the world community.

A new economic order is needed to structure more equitable relationships between people in the areas of trade and finance. Pope Paul VI clearly called for this in his encyclical *On the Progress of Peoples (Populorum Progressio)* in 1967, and Pope John Paul II has reiterated this point on several occasions, including his encyclical *On the Hundredth Anniversary of Rerum Novarum (Centisimus Annus)* in 1991. The rapid development in our own time of a global economic system may have the inevitable effect of some movement toward equalization of incomes worldwide, but the actions of the developed countries and of the multinational corporations that dominate the market need to be viewed in light of the basic rights of all people to the necessities of life.

Questions of environmental protection also need to be addressed on a multinational basis, so that corporations act responsibly toward the environment even when no one particular country can regulate their global activities. At a Vatican conference on October 22, 1993, Pope John Paul II denounced the practice of international companies that use poor countries as dumping grounds for hazardous waste and as sites for environmentally unsafe plants. The side agreements negotiated as part of the North American Free Trade Act are a step in the right direction, but much more can and should be done to protect the environment around the world.

On a more personal level, those who care about the environment need to examine their own personal lifestyle and patterns of consumption. St. Elizabeth Ann Seton, the first person born in the United States to be canonized, advised her followers to "live simply so others can simply live." If we are serious about sharing the world's resources with all people, we will need to adopt a simpler lifestyle ourselves. The Vatican nuncio to the United Nations, Archbishop Renato Martino, noted on November 23, 1993, that there has been little more than lip service given to the call for nations to change their pattern of consumption issued by the United Nations Conference on the Environment and Development in Rio de Janeiro in 1992. Changes in national patterns of consumption will occur only when enough individuals in those nations adopt a simpler style of life.

The Religion of Consumerism

Such changes, of course, will always be difficult for a culture that has made conspicuous consumption its idol and the shopping mall its cathedral. An editorial cartoon by Mike Thompson shows a father and son next to the Christmas tree. The father is saying, "Son, I hope all the hype and hoopla surrounding Christmas hasn't diminished your belief in the religion we worship during this season." The son answers, "No, I still believe in consumerism."

In our area we recently saw the opening of one of the few new malls to be developed in the country that year, and it was the lead story in the papers and on the news for weeks. The representatives of the media know where our culture's real values lie. For many in our culture, shopping is truly an addiction. Those who seek to live their faith and to preserve the environment may need to join "Consumers Anonymous" to break the hold of our cultural penchant for buying and owning everything in sight.

The Christian Counterculture

Our experience of liturgy invites us to worship a different God and to adopt a countercultural set of values to shape our lives. The Scriptures we hear at Mass frequently exhort us to give to the poor and to put God above material wealth. We are continually confronted with the example of Jesus himself, who lived lightly on the earth and warned his followers not to be enticed by the lure of wealth. Our sharing in the Eucharist calls us to a more equitable sharing of the world's goods with all people.

In adopting a simpler lifestyle, we need to have a conviction that the quality of our lives is not determined simply by how much we own or consume. There is more to life than the material, and we affirm that truth every time we worship the Lord. Our donations at the collection express our conviction that life is about more than the accumulation of wealth. The relationships that bind us to one another in the worshiping assembly teach us that love is deeper than the divisions that wealth and status create. Our sharing in the Eucharistic meal reminds us that sharing God's gifts in love is the core of the meaning of our lives. And our continual use of material things in worship as sacraments of God's presence reminds us of the proper approach to the use of all of creation.

So many environmental problems result from our excessive consumption of material resources. Our overconsumption of meat has led to cutting much of the tropical rain forest to provide grazing land for more cattle. Our wasteful use of oil, gas, and coal is intensifying the greenhouse effect and producing acid rain. The use of fluorocarbons in refrigerants and plastics is resulting in the depletion of the ozone layer. Our industrial might and economic success have often been based on the use of toxic chemicals that now pollute our air and land and water. Planned obsolescence by manufacturers encourages even more consumption while contributing to our growing problems with waste disposal. Though recycling is beginning to recover some of the resources we use, most of them end up in the waste stream, so we can buy and consume some more. Simply put, we who live in the developed countries consume too much.

We overconsume in large measure in a desperate attempt to establish our importance and value as persons and to assure our comfort and security. We need to live out our conviction that we are important in God's eyes simply because God made us and loves us. We do not establish our self-importance by what we own. And we cannot find true security in material things, no matter how much we amass. Our security must lie in God's love, which is where the liturgy posits it every time we engage in the act of worship.

Pope John Paul II's *Centisimus Annus*

Pope John Paul II stressed the links between consumerism and the ecological question in his encyclical *On the Hundredth Anniversary of Rerum Novarum (Centesimus Annus),* issued to commemorate one hundred years of Catholic social teachings. Despite the noninclusive style of the translation, it is worth quoting the pontiff at some length:

> It is not wrong to want to live better; what is wrong is a style of life which is presumed to be better when it is directed toward "having" rather than "being," and which wants to have more, not in order to be more, but in order to spend life in enjoyment as an end in itself. . . . Equally worrying is the ecological question which accompanies the problem of consumerism and which is closely connected to it. In his desire to have and to enjoy rather than to be and to grow, man consumes the resources of the earth and his own life in an excessive and disordered way. . . . Man thinks that he can make arbitrary use of the earth, subjecting it without restraint to his will, as though it did not have its own requisites and a prior God-given purpose, which man can indeed develop but must not betray. Instead of carrying out his role as a cooperator with God in the work of creation, man sets himself up in place of God and thus ends up provoking a rebellion on the part of nature.[3]

---

3. *On the Hundredth Anniversary of Rerum Novarum* (Washington: United States Catholic Conference, 1991) nos. 36, 37.

Proper care of the environment requires a lifestyle that does not draw its sense of worth from consumerism. There is a bumper sticker that reads: "The one who dies with the most toys wins." That is not what the gospel teaches, nor is it what the liturgy celebrates. The Christian believes that the one who dies with the most love wins.

Questions for Reflection and Discussion

1. Of all the social justice issues discussed in this chapter, which one do you think has the most effect on the environment?

2. Can you name effects on the environment that have resulted from wars in your lifetime? Do peace activists and environmental activists have common cause? Does the liturgy help you to become a more peaceful person?

3. How does poverty affect the environment? Can you name places in the world today where the need for survival forces people into nonsustainable practices? How do we start to create a more equitable sharing of the goods of the earth?

4. Do you agree that we need to adopt a simpler lifestyle in this country? What concrete steps can you take in your own life to live more simply so that others may simply live?

5. Is consumerism the real American religion? How much does it affect your own life? Do the things we own really make us happy?

6. What does the gospel teach us about possessions and about sharing? How can we set ourselves free from the addiction to buy and to own?

Chapter Seven

The Ecology of Worship

At the annual meeting of members of a small church, it was suggested that a drive be started to buy a chandelier for the church. This suggestion drew much support from the assembly. One elderly member rose to speak, however, and objected to the idea. "It's extravagant and wasteful," he insisted. "Not only will it cost a fortune to buy the fool thing and install it, then we'll have to find money to hire somebody who can play it!"

We have focused mostly so far on the effect that worship can have in shaping and nurturing a deeper ecological awareness, but the interaction is bidirectional. Besides considering ways to include ecology *in* worship, it is valuable to consider the ecology *of* worship. Just as worship has much to contribute to shaping a healthy ecological awareness, so there is much that a heightened awareness of the environment can contribute to the worship life of the church community.

The first gift that an ecological awareness brings to worship is simply the basic recognition that the environment in which we worship matters. Just as we are influenced in a thousand different ways by our links to the natural and manmade environment in which we live, so too our experience of worship is significantly influenced by a variety of factors in the worship environment. We are becoming increasingly aware of the impact on our productivity, our health, and our happiness that is exerted by the natural and human environments in which we live and work. A similar awareness is needed about the effects of the environment in which we worship.

When the liturgical renewal after Vatican II began, it was accompanied by a broad mandate for renewal of all elements of the life of the Church. Part of this involved serious reevaluation of the purpose of the Church itself and of the mission to which the Church is called. One of the positive signs of renewal is an increased awareness of the Church's obligation to care for the poor and the needy of the world. For many Catholics in this country, involvement in anti-poverty programs and work for social justice meant a radical change in their earlier understanding of what it meant to be Catholic. A Church that had been largely turned inward, caring for Catholic immigrants and defending the true faith against outsiders, began to turn more and more outward and became more involved in the needs of the world.

In those heady days right after the council, this awareness of the needs of the poor was often viewed in contrast to the ritual life of the Church. Some saw a fundamental opposition between the Church at worship (the Church in the sanctuary) and the Church serving those in need (the Church in the world). Clergy and seminarians were categorized as to whether they were oriented to the sanctuary or the world. Those who manifested a concern for the Church's worship and sacramental life were often derided for living in the past.

Concern for the poor also led to questioning expenditures for ornate and sometimes ostentatious worship spaces. The excesses of the past led some to reject all church art and decoration as unnecessary. They insisted that Christians could worship just as well in a barn as they could in an ornate chapel. This impulse coincided with a movement toward simplicity and functionality in the architectural world. While this led to many new worship spaces that are beautiful in their simplicity, the desire to minimize expenditures sometimes led to new or renovated spaces that were quite bare and even barren.

While true simplicity and functionality are quite appropriate for worship spaces, sometimes too little attention was paid to the effect of the worship environment on the experience of worship itself. The spaces in which we humans gather and function significantly shape the experiences we have there. A space can be warm or cold, both physically and psychically. It can be intimate or overwhelming in size. The sounds and smells in the space can invite or intimidate. Even the arrangement of the furniture conditions our expectations and our actions. If I enter a room with chairs all lined up in rows facing a podium, for example, I expect a different experience than when I enter a room with all the chairs in a circle.

Awareness of the extent and pervasive nature of the effect of the surroundings on worship has grown in recent years. A landmark in this progress was the document *Environment and Art in Catholic Worship,* issued by the Bishops' Committee on the Liturgy of the National Conference of Catholic Bishops in 1978. This document was later endorsed by the full conference of bishops as the official guidelines for art and environment in an appendix to the General Instruction of the Roman Missal. This work has educated many to the influence of art and environment on the worship experience, and thus to the importance of careful attention to the whole environment of worship.

By environment the document means "the larger space in which the action of the assembly takes place. At its broadest, it is the setting of the building in its neighborhood, including outdoor spaces. More specifically it means the character of a specific space and how it affects the assembly. There are elements in the environment, therefore, which contribute to the overall experience, e.g., the seating arrangement, the placement of liturgical centers of action, temporary decoration, light, acoustics, spaciousness, etc."[1]

The document notes that "liturgical celebrations of the faith community involve the whole person. They are not purely religious or merely rational and intellectual exercises, but also human experiences calling on all human faculties: body, mind, sense, imagination, emotions, memory. Attention to these is one of the urgent needs of contemporary liturgical renewal" (no. 5). Our heightened ecological awareness reminds us that the human person is constantly affected by a multiplicity of factors in the environment. Good worship re-

1. Bishops' Committee on the Liturgy, *Environment and Art in Catholic Worship* (Washington: National Conference of Catholic Bishops, 1978) no. 24.

quires paying attention to these various factors and fostering an environment conducive to prayer and celebration.

The document says that a "simple and attractive beauty in everything that is used or done in liturgy is the most effective invitation to this kind of experience. One should be able to sense something special (and nothing trivial) in everything that is seen and heard, touched and smelled, and tasted in liturgy" (no. 12). This kind of care and sensitivity is still uncommon, but it should mark all our decisions about every dimension of the worship environment.

Architecture

One of the most obvious factors shaping the worship environment is the size and shape of the building itself. In the past, churches and cathedrals were often built with the goal of creating a monumental edifice as a tribute to God and to impress the worshipers with God's greatness. A common effect on those who enter such a space is to make them feel insignificant and overwhelmed. This was in accord with a liturgy that was performed by the clergy while the "insignificant" laity watched or said other prayers.

The requirements for good liturgy today are different. The renewed liturgy needs the whole assembly to take its rightful place as the "celebrants" of worship. In union with the priest, the assembly as a whole joins in the worship Christ offers to the Father. The scale of the worship space should make the worshiper feel welcome and important as a member of the people of God gathered to worship their Lord.

Obviously, the size of the space must be related to the size of the assembly itself. Since our worship assemblies range from hundreds on Sundays to a handful on weekdays, the need for alternate spaces or flexible spaces becomes apparent. It is still far too common to find weekday assemblies of a dozen or less spread out in a space that will seat a thousand. Such a space makes the formation of a true assembly for worship difficult at best. Smaller, more intimate spaces are needed for small-group worship.

The style and focus of the space are also crucial for good liturgy. In the recent past, most Catholic churches were designed as shrines for the tabernacle. The attention, both visually and spiritually, was on the reserved Sacrament as a focal point for devotion. Other religious art was added to foster devotion to the saints, to Christ in his passion, to the infant Jesus, etc. These items were useful in the liturgical space because the assembly was not directly involved in the worship itself and turned to various devotional prayers while the clergy celebrated the liturgy.

The recovery of the central role of the assembly in worship requires a different style and focus. The focal points are the central places where the worship action itself occurs: the altar, the ambo or lectern, and the presider's chair. The space should help the assembly be aware of itself as the gathered body of Christ and foster attention to the action of the liturgy. Thus many devotional elements that were appropriate in the past become distractions and obstacles to full participation today.

Since the celebration of the Eucharist is the focus of the assembly, the reserved Sacrament in the tabernacle should be in a different space, one designed for individual devotion. As *Environment and Art in Catholic Worship* notes, "a room or chapel specifically designed and separate from the major space is important so that no confusion can take place between the celebration of the eucharist and reservation" (no. 78). This enables the assembly gathered for worship to focus on Christ's presence in the various modes enunciated by the Constitution on the Sacred Liturgy of Vatican II: in the assembly itself, through the priest, in the word proclaimed, and in the bread and wine shared.

Design of the worship space should facilitate attention to each of these presences. Natural sight lines should provide easy attention to the altar, the ambo, and the presider's chair, and members of the assembly ought to be naturally aware of other members gathered with them. Often a semicircular or fan-shaped design is used to foster the assembly's awareness of one another, though other arrangements are also possible.

Another issue in many churches is accessibility for those with limited mobility. The Americans with Disabilities Act requires such accessibility in all public spaces, but churches should have been leading the way in taking steps to make worship available to all members of the community.

Lighting and Sound

Within the worship space, attention must be given to the factors that enable or inhibit the full participation by the assembly in the action of the liturgy. Two of the most basic factors are lighting and sound communication. Many older churches are dimly lit, frustrating worshipers who try to join in hymns and prayers but cannot see clearly enough to read. This is an increasing problem as both our society and our assemblies increase in age and decrease in visual acuity.

Light is a powerful element in the worship space. Even beyond its functional value for reading, a brightly lit church encourages a more joyful and hopeful atmosphere. We all know the effect of a bright sunny day in contrast to that of an overcast, dreary one. A fully lit worship space is generally more appropriate for Sunday worship than a dim and dreary atmosphere. Flexible lighting, however, also enables changing the mood for different types of worship and for different moments in the worship. Light might focus strongly on the ambo when the word of God is proclaimed, for example, while the other lights are dimmed to encourage attention to the proclamation itself. When the action moves to the altar, more light might be directed there. At a penance service, light might be more subdued during times for reflection and examination of conscience.

Inadequate sound systems are another obstacle to good worship in many churches. Our aging population should also prompt us to pay more attention to the quality of sound reproduction during worship. If the lector cannot be heard or the celebrant's voice is muffled, the assembly's participation is impeded. With all the advances made in sound technology in recent years, there is no good excuse for inadequate sound systems in our worship spaces. Good systems are not cheap, and an acoustical engineer may be needed to determine the best use of technology, but whatever is done to make it easy for the assembly to hear the ministers and one another is money well spent.

With our aging culture, more and more people are living with impaired hearing. Systems are available to provide individual acoustic amplification for those who need it. Such systems are not overly expensive and speak volumes about our commitment to full participation in worship by all members of the community.

Acoustical experts should also be consulted if there is any consideration of carpeting a worship space. Though carpet can convey a certain warmth and comfort, it often dulls the sound qualities of a space. This can be devastating for music and can also inhibit the assembly's participation; if people cannot hear one another singing or praying aloud, they are less likely to join in wholeheartedly themselves. Some argue that churches should never be carpeted, so that hard surfaces may allow sound to reverberate fully. At the very least, any decision to install carpet should be considered carefully with the guidance of acoustical engineers and musicians.

Music and Silence

In the realm of sound, music is a crucial environmental factor in worship. Good music is a vital factor in creating an atmosphere of prayer and celebration. We are still learning, in the Catholic tradition, how best to use music within worship. The musical repertoire for Catholic worship has grown rapidly since the council, and much good music is available, both contemporary compositions and treasures from the tradition. But Catholic parishes are often "pikers" when it comes to salaries allocated for music ministers. If we want to have good music ministry, we must value it enough to pay just salaries. Only then can we expect instrumental and liturgical competence appropriate for the worship of God.

Silence, too, is an important part of the worship environment. Just as noise pollution in our cities makes people long for the quiet of a walk in the woods, so the constancy of noise in modern life in general should make us more aware of the need for silence. This may seem at first to be in tension with the principle of active participation and the use of music throughout our worship, but silence is an integral part of the ritual, too. There is a pattern to worship, with times for song, times for vocal prayer, and times for silence. Attention to the inherent rhythm in the liturgical act is crucial for a prayerful worship experience. Many assemblies need to recover the ability to enter into shared, prayerful silence.

Visual Art

When it comes to the visual environment, we can learn much from our own tradition. Through much of our history, the Catholic Church was the patron of the arts. From popes to local church communities, the Church encouraged artists to dedicate their best efforts to the glory of God. Much of the great art in the culture of Europe during the last two millennia was produced under the auspices of the Church.

In more recent years, however, we have been content with the cheap and the tawdry. What has passed for art in many of our churches has been mass-produced plaster statues with sloppy and garish paint jobs. We have settled for poor imitations of real art rather than paying for true works of beauty and creativity. There is a great need for us to recover our tradition of using only the best of human creativity in our worship. Good art does not have to be extravagant or ornate, but it does have to be authentic and of good quality.

Those same two criteria can be applied to everything that is used in worship: vessels, candles, flowers, bread, wine, vestments, and even the materials used to construct the altar, the ambo, and the presider's chair. All the materials used should be authentic and of good quality. Recent years have seen some atrocious violations of this basic principle. Some churches have resorted to using plastic candle shells with oil canisters inside rather than using real candles that burn down and remind us to give our life for the glory of God. Other parishes use artificial flowers or plants so that they will never wilt or die. Neither fake candles nor fake flowers are ever appropriate for worship. So, too, fake marble altars or plastic-laminated ambos that look like wood are inappropriate. Wood should look like wood, and marble should look like marble.

The use of authentic materials is crucial if worship is to foster a truly contemplative approach to life. While there is room for contemplative appreciation for human artifacts, contemplating a plastic flower does not approach the experience of the real thing. When flowers are not in season, dried flower arrangements are still authentic and natural. A deeper sense of the value of the various elements of creation, flowing from a more developed ecological awareness, can help us recognize the importance of using created elements honestly and reverently in our worship.

The Sense of Smell and Movement

Another powerful factor in our environment is the sense of smell. The smell of salt air near the ocean or the musty scent of decaying leaves on a walk through woods in autumn can bring back a host of memories and emotions. The sense of smell is one of the most powerful triggers of memories and moods in the human psyche. Attention to this sense in worship has been often overlooked in recent years. The long tradition of using incense during worship attests to the importance of involving all the senses in the liturgy. Other scents, too, influence us at worship: evergreens at Christmas, lilies at Easter, the odor of candle wax, the sweet scent of the chrism used at baptism, confirmation, and ordination, etc. All are important in creating an appropriate atmosphere for prayer and celebration.

Another sense that should be involved in worship is a sense of movement. Our liturgical tradition includes a variety of postures for worship, as well as various processions and even dances. We need to relearn how to use movement within worship more effectively. Processions, for example, are supposed to go from one place to another, not just wander around a circle and end up where they began. They can be done with grace and style and spacing of ministers, so that they approximate a reverent dance rather than looking like a crowd rushing to get in or out.

Movement in worship should not be limited just to the special ministers, however, but should often involve the whole assembly. One of the major impediments to authentic movement in worship today is the existence of pews. One could hardly imagine a more inhibiting design for filling a space and preventing more than minimal movement. It is true that pews offer maximum seating capacity in a given area, but many communities would be better off with less capacity and more flexibility. Even using some movable seating in the area of the church closest to the altar would allow for flexible arrangements and more possibility of movement on various occasions.

The Human Environment

Often overlooked in considering the worship environment is the human factor, yet this is the most important element in the environment. To ignore it is like trying to understand our natural environment without taking account of the impact that humans have on the ecology of the world.

The importance of the human factor becomes obvious to many people when they enter a contemporary church building that is unoccupied at the time. A frequent complaint is that the building looks so empty. Something essential is missing without the human assembly. It is the assembly that most significantly shapes the environment for worship.

Many assemblies still need to learn the importance of their role. Their first task is simply to form an assembly, which involves both physical and social aspects. When people enter the church and scatter themselves around a space much larger than they can fill, they physically prevent the formation of a unified assembly ready to worship together. But even if they are in close physical proximity in a crowded church, it will not be a true assembly for worship unless there is an openness to one another that allows them to form one body and to sing and pray with one voice and one heart.

The issue here might simply be called hospitality. An assembly that has learned to be hospitable has learned to recognize the presence of Christ in one another and in their gathering. "Where two or three are gathered in my name," Jesus said, "there am I in their midst." A deeper incarnational awareness is essential to the recovery of the full role of the assembly in worship. If we were more attuned to the signs of God throughout creation, we might be more aware of the presence of Christ in our brothers and sisters as well.

Our worshiping assemblies will not reach their full potential until all those who come to worship recognize their responsibility for creating a proper environment for common prayer and celebration. Too many people assume that creating this environment is the task of the presider and other special liturgical ministers. In fact, the assembly itself is the most influential factor in the environment. Good presiders and ministers can help, but only the assembly can create an atmosphere that is hospitable for worship.

Learning to do this will require a basic change in approach for many Catholics. Before Vatican II we were well trained to approach worship as a fairly private matter between ourselves and God. We were taught not to look at others or to talk to them in church; our attention was to be on God alone. The renewal of the liturgy has reminded us that worship is a communal action; this requires a near reversal of what many of us learned as children. To enter into one communal act of worship, which is what liturgy requires, is very different from coming to church for a time of quiet, individual prayer. That is another reason why the reserved Sacrament in the tabernacle should be in a separate space appropriate for private prayer rather than in the main assembly space where people need to be greeting one another and recognizing Christ in their midst.

Making this shift is more difficult because of the strong current of individualism in our culture. As we noted in Chapter Two (see p. 17), our culture puts great emphasis on protecting individual rights and fostering individual freedom and initiative. More than any other civilization in the history of humanity, we have exalted the individual, and this is a gift we offer to the world.

But like any good thing, this focus on the individual can be overdone. In recent decades we have engaged in a hyperindividualism that leaves little room for common values or common action. In entertainment, in books, in politics, in business, in sports, and even in religion, we have been deluged with advice to seek self-fulfillment, self-improvement, self-aggrandizement. We have been urged to "look out for number one," to "be all that you can be," to "go for the gusto," to "vote your pocketbook," to put self first above all else. Selfishness and greed have been extolled as virtues rather than vices. And sacrifice for the common good is almost a novel idea these days.

Yet sacrifice for the common good is a basic principle of Christianity and a basic prerequisite for worship. Our worship is a symbol of our life. Just as none of us gets exactly what we want in any communal situation (family, work, club), so none of us gets exactly the worship we would like. I may not get the musician I prefer or the presider I like best. I may prefer other songs or be in the mood for a different style of homily. To enter into a common act means to surrender individual desires and individual control in order to function as a community. Community always requires compromise and self-surrender, whether that community is the family, the neighborhood, the Church, the nation, or the world community. Respect for the individual is important, but the individual is also part of a community, and in worship the community is the principal actor.

An ecological mindset can help here if it teaches us that we are always linked to others in our environment and that we influence one another for good or for ill. As Professor James Withey of Notre Dame puts it, "You are somebody else's environment."[2] Learning to worship as one assembly united in Christ is perhaps the biggest challenge facing the ongoing liturgical renewal. Learning to do so is important, however, both for worship and for other areas of our life. Facing our responsibilities to the common good and being willing to compromise our own desires for the sake of the community is essential to healthy human life. It is also clearly essential to action to preserve the environment of the planet.

Questions for Reflection and Discussion

1. Think of various church buildings in which you have worshiped. How did the environment of those worship spaces affect you? Are any of those spaces more conducive to worship for you? Why?

2. Quoted by Edward Fisher in *Notre Dame Magazine* (summer 1988) 77.

2. What does the architecture of your parish church say about the community that worships there? How does it shape the experience of worship? What are the focal points that draw one's attention? Is your church accessible to all?

3. How is the lighting in your normal worship space? If it needs improvement, what is needed? How is the sound system? Have provisions been made for the hearing impaired?

4. How is the music for worship in your parish? Can you think of times when the music really made the worship come alive? Does your parish pay musicians an adequate wage? If not, what can be done?

5. How well does your community enter into shared silence? Is there a healthy pause after each reading and after the homily? Is there a time for reflection after communion?

6. What kind of art is in your church building? Are all the items used in worship authentic and beautiful?

7. How much attention is given to the sense of smell in your parish worship? How much is movement part of your worship? Are movements and gestures done with grace and style?

8. How would you describe the "human environment" of your parish liturgy? Is the assembly hospitable? Does the assembly know and accept its essential role in making good worship happen?

9. How often have you been aware of the presence of Christ in the assembly gathered for worship? How can we become more aware of his presence in every member of the body of Christ?

10. What does the idea of sacrifice mean to you? How is it part of your worship experience? Is the celebration of the Eucharist a sharing in the sacrifice of Christ?

Chapter Eight

Some Practical Suggestions

There is a wonderful film called "The Man Who Planted Trees," which recounts the life of a French shepherd named Elezard Bouffier. He lived in Provence at the beginning of the century and tended his flocks in a rather barren area. As he moved about with his sheep each autumn, he collected acorns that had fallen from the few trees in the area. Then in the spring he would punch holes in the ground with his shepherd's staff and drop the acorns in them. He did this for thirty-seven years, and by the time he died in 1947, the once barren countryside was covered with trees and the forests teemed with wildlife.

Most of us may not have such a dramatic impact on the environment, but Bouffier's story reminds us of the potential of even small actions to have a cumulative impact. This chapter offers a few suggestions that might begin to express a deeper commitment to the care of the environment and the development of Christian worship.

These suggestions aim at fostering a healthy interplay between worship and awareness of the environment. They are not meant to be exhaustive but rather suggestive of the ways that these two movements can enrich one another. Those who seek to be attentive both to the needs of the environment and the dynamics of worship will find that they continually discover new ways in which these two worlds interact.

Not Misusing Liturgy

Focusing on the connections between ecology and liturgy naturally raises the question of how our concern about the natural environment can be brought into the community's worship.

71

Great caution and sensitivity to the nature of liturgy are necessary here. There is a great temptation to "use" worship as a tool
to promote a political and social agenda. This same temptation
occurs with any issue of importance in contemporary life: abortion, mission work, the needs of retired religious, anti-poverty
programs, racism, sexism, and a host of other concerns.

The key is to understand how liturgy teaches and forms
us. The liturgy is a very powerful teacher. The way we worship shapes who we are, both as individuals and as a people,
but it does not accomplish this in a direct and heavy-handed
fashion. The experience of worship shapes us much more sub-
tly and gradually than a political speech or a classroom exer-
cise. Because it works at a much deeper and more subtle level,
the liturgy can form us more powerfully and more deeply
than these other approaches.

The liturgy forms us by gradually shaping our attitudes
and emotions toward basic realities of life. The experience of
worship plants in our minds and hearts images of how life can
be or, more accurately, how things really are in God's sight.
These images, planted repeatedly over time, begin to reshape
our attitudes and thus to recast our emotions toward God, toward self, toward other people, and toward all of creation.
And once our emotions have changed, our behavior changes
as well. This is the way worship fosters conversion, the gradual giving over of our whole life to God.

This mode of formation or education is powerful, but it is
less direct and therefore perhaps less satisfying to those who
want immediate results. But the liturgy is not a tool to be used
to promote any particular political or social agenda, no matter
how worthwhile. To subordinate the liturgy to other purposes
is to reverse the proper order of things. Liturgy is celebrated to
worship God; it is an act of contemplation. The effects that it
has on the participants are a side benefit, not the purpose of
worship. To turn liturgy into a tool for something else violates
its fundamental meaning.

More Attention to Symbols

"The topic for today's class essay," announced the teacher,
"is the most beautiful thing you ever saw." One student

thought for a moment, wrote briefly, and then handed in his paper. On it he had written, "The most beautiful thing I ever saw was too beautiful for words."

Recognizing that worship affects us by placing images in our minds and hearts might also remind us that liturgy, like all ritual celebration, relies heavily on symbols. Rituals can be understood as a skein of symbols, strung together in a pattern that expresses meanings which transcend the power of words to contain. Symbols are crucial to human communication on a deep level. When we want to express the mysteries of life, we rely on symbols because words are inadequate.

Those who promote ecological awareness know the power of symbols. Whether it is a blue whale, a spotted owl, a penguin, a bald eagle, or any other representative of the natural world, such creatures become symbols that call forth emotion and commitment. Those who are responsible for preparing worship should be even more aware of the power of symbols and the necessity of using them fully. If liturgy is to foster a contemplative approach to life and creation, then the things we use and the actions we do in worship should be handled in such a way that their reality is abundantly apparent. Only with difficulty can an assembly be called to contemplate the meaning of bread or wine or oil or water if these things are used in a perfunctory and minimal fashion. Our penchant for efficiency and economy has led us to skimp so much on worship materials for so long that many people may not even realize how deprived their worship experience has become.

Within our worship, much more attention should be paid to the basic symbols we use. The bread for the Eucharistic meal should be bread that can be broken and shared. Ideally, it should be bread prepared by members of the assembly. The wine, too, should be the best we can provide. The vessels used to hold both of these symbols should be both beautiful and cherished. They may be made of various materials, but they should be worthy and dignified pieces.

Since the Mass is a meal, the bread and wine used for communion should be the bread and wine consecrated at that Mass. The continued use of leftover hosts from the tabernacle at every Mass is a clear signal that those responsible for worship are not sensitive to the power of symbols and the real meaning of the Eucharistic meal shared by the assembly. We would never think of serving leftovers as a matter of course when we have dinner guests; an authentic ritual meal demands at least as much care and dignity as a dinner party. The reserved Sacrament is kept for the sick, not for regular use at the assembly's worship. It will be necessary periodically, of course, to consume extra hosts that may accumulate over several Masses, but this should be clearly the exceptional case and not the rule for every Mass.

The water used for baptism should be used in abundance. The full symbol is baptism by immersion, and fonts should be renovated to provide for this fuller use of water. If baptism is done by pouring, then the water should be used fully enough for the assembly to see and hear the water as it is poured. Perhaps if we were more sensitive to the gift of water in our worship, we might be more strongly committed to protecting this natural resource from pollution and wasteful use.

In a similar fashion, all the symbols we use in worship need to be used more fully and more richly. The oil for catechumens, the oil for anointing the sick, and the chrism for confirmation and ordination should be used abundantly and should not be wiped off. The scent of the chrism, especially, should fill the worship space. Incense should be used in great clouds; if people find it unpleasant, that may be an indication that we need to find a better incense, even if it costs a bit more. Movements and gestures in liturgy should be done as fully and gracefully as possible so that they may be both beautiful and prayerful.

Authentic Materials for Worship

If contemplation is the approach we wish to take to the world around us, then everything that we use in our lives is valued for what it truly is. In worship especially, we should make sure that what we do and what we use is authentic; there is no room here for what is phony or fake. There is the tendency to let our modern technology reign supreme. We can make plastic or silk flowers that "almost look real." But a plastic flower does not wilt and fade, which is part of the reality of flowers. When Jesus speaks of the flowers of the field that wither and die, he wasn't talking about plastic! A plastic shell with an oil canister inside may look like a candle, but a real candle burns itself down, giving its life to the praise of God. Plastic imitations do not suggest this symbolism, nor do electric vigil lights. In furnishings, too, authentic materials should be used. A marble altar can be a beautiful work of art. So can a wooden altar. But a wooden altar covered with plastic laminate to look like marble is a sham and unworthy of our worship.

There may be rare cases where an exception must be made to this basic principle. Fire codes in many localities, for example, do not allow real Christmas trees in public buildings, including churches, so we may be forced to use an artificial tree if we want trees at all. Of course, we might find other ways to decorate at Christmas, but in any case such exceptions should be rare. Authentic materials should be used whenever it is possible to do so.

Celebrating Earth, Water, Air

Using authentic materials and symbols fully and richly will help us to appreciate the gift that these elements of creation are. Beyond their normal use, however, there is value in periodically focusing on these gifts in a fuller way in worship. Some rural parishes, for example, invite farm families to bring a container of soil from their farms to church to be blessed and then returned to the farm as a reminder that the soil is a gift to be cherished and conserved. Urban and suburban parishes might do something similar for those who raise gardens.

A prayer service focused on the gift of water could combine baptismal themes with prayer for an end to water pollution and thanksgiving for the gift of water. This might be especially welcome in areas where water supplies are very limited, for example, the American Southwest, but it is no less appropriate where water is abundant.

In a similar way, we might at times focus on the gift of air to breathe and pray for a decrease in the pollution of the atmosphere while we thank God for the breath of life.

Any of these elements might be celebrated in a special prayer service, or prayers for the conservation of these gifts might be included in the general intercessions at Mass occasionally. Other less obvious attention given to the elements may also nurture a respect for the environment. Water kept visible in a baptismal font with continually flowing water can speak a constant message of the value of this gift, for example.

The American bishops have approved a number of new Mass formularies for the new Sacramentary, among which is one for "The Reverent Use of Creation." If approved by Rome, these Mass texts may be used on any day that votive Masses are permitted.

Rogation Days and Other Annual Observances

Attention to the land and to the harvest was a regular part of Catholic worship in centuries past. The Rogation Days, celebrated since the fifth century on the three days preceding Ascension Thursday, were days of prayer for a fruitful harvest and for protection from famine and hunger. April 25 (later also the date of the feast of St. Mark) was also designated as a Rogation Day around the beginning of the seventh century.

The Rogation Days are not listed in the current calendar, in part because they conflict somewhat with the Easter season. But they live on in a new form in this country in the Soil and Water Stewardship Week sponsored by the National Association of Conservation Districts. It is observed every year from the last Sunday in April to the first Sunday in May. Since this is within the Fifty Days of Easter, this observance should not have the penitential character that sometimes marked Rogation Days, but it offers a good time to celebrate the gifts of soil and water and to pray for their proper use and conservation. This might be linked to the Easter focus on the "new creation" that has begun with the Resurrection.

Earth Day is observed each year on April 22 and World Environment Day on June 5. In connection with the latter, the first weekend in June is designated each year as Environmental Sabbath. As we noted earlier, care should be taken not to misuse the liturgy to promote a cause, but we can celebrate God's gifts without turning worship into a soapbox.

Rural Life Masses

Many dioceses with a significant rural population have special Masses, often with the bishop presiding, in connection with the spring planting or the fall harvest. Such Masses, gathering people from a cluster of rural parishes, offer the opportunity to support farmers and farm workers, to praise God for the gifts of creation, to pray for a good harvest, and to affirm good conservation practices as a moral responsibility.

Those who live in rural communities, however, often note that people who live in the cities need to recognize the importance of these issues as well. Perhaps even parishes in the center city need to find ways to celebrate the gift of food that God gives to us and to recognize and pray for those who produce the food. Those who live in the city are no less dependent on good harvests than those who farm the land; they are just generally not as aware of the fact. The use of good bread and wine in our worship might lead us to celebrate the gift of nourishment in special ways from time to time.

Many parishes have discovered that people will come to church in large numbers on Thanksgiving Day. Such a celebration offers an ideal time to give thanks for the harvest, but the opportunity is often overlooked in favor of a more general theme of gratitude. Thanksgiving is the American harvest feast. That fact should be reflected not only in decor (baskets of produce, etc.) but also in the homily, in the intercessions, and perhaps in the choice of prayers and readings among those offered. Some parishes have developed a custom of giving a loaf of bread to each family at Mass that day to be used with their Thanksgiving meal. This simple gesture is a wonderful reminder of God's goodness and a natural link with the use of bread in the Eucharistic meal, which is always a thanksgiving meal.

The Feast of St. Francis

Long before Pope John Paul II called St. Francis of Assisi the patron of ecology, many Christians recognized his love of nature and his attitude of respect for creation. His feast day on October 4 offers another ideal opportunity for celebrating our integral relationship with the rest of creation. Many parishes offer a blessing of animals on this day. Though there is perhaps a danger of gimmickry in this custom, it can be a valid and prayerful way to observe the feast. But Francis also recognized the sun, the moon, and the earth as brothers and sisters. Our celebration of his feast should not be limited to a focus on animals but can remind us of the respect we owe to every part of God's creation. Those who are directly involved in conservation and recycling efforts might be especially invited to an evening Mass or Evening Prayer on this feast to find nourishment in common worship and common commitment.

Celebrating the feast day of St. Francis should also remind us of the importance of social justice in preserving the environment. Francis lived a life of radical poverty and saw his embrace of Lady Poverty, as he called her, as central to his following of Christ. That kind of radical simplicity of life made few demands on the earth's resources and also led Francis to a constant concern for those in need. He insisted that his followers should own nothing and should always trust in God's providence for their needs. Such a stance leads to a constant sense of dependence on God and a constant sense of gratitude for all that we have received.

Pro-Life Month

The feast of St. Francis falls in October, the same month that is observed by Catholic parishes in the United States as pro-life month. The materials issued from the United States Catholic Conference always suggest attention to a variety of life issues, including, but not limited to, abortion. The Holy Father and the Philippine bishops have both called ecology a fundamental pro-life issue; it should be included in this observance. Destruction of the world by pollution can lead to a devastation no less thorough than nuclear destruction. If human life is to survive on this planet, ecological issues must be addressed. This is perhaps the most basic reason that ecology is a moral issue.

October 16 is World Food Day, another observance that could be highlighted.

A Penitential Service Focused on Ecology

Perhaps during pro-life month or at some other time of the year, a parish might celebrate a penitential service focused on ecology. Though most parishes use penance services only during Advent and Lent to provide for seasonal confessions, the Rite of Penance encourages other penitential gatherings with or without individual confession. Even to schedule such a gathering would give a clear signal to parishioners that ecology is a moral issue and that our continuing wastefulness and pollution of the environment are sinful and must stop.

The General Intercessions

In a similar way, periodic inclusion of petitions about ecological issues in the general intercessions at Sunday Mass both signals the importance of these issues and reminds us that we need the help of the Lord to solve the problems we face. Care must be taken not to "use" the petitions to chastise people or "beat them over the head" with an agenda. Petitions must be composed as true prayers in which the whole assembly can join.

Creation Covenant

The following "Creation Covenant" was published in *Maryknoll* magazine. It might be used in a prayer service and/or published in the parish bulletin.

We covenant this day with all creation
with what was, is and will be;
With every living creature
those that sustain us and those we sustain;
With all that moves upon the earth
and with the earth itself;
With all that lives in the water
and with the water itself;
With all that flies through the air
and with the air itself.
We confess that our own kind
has put all creation at risk.
We mark our covenant by the rainbow
as our pledge never again
to destroy creation through our greed,

our negligence, our selfishness
and our sins.
Remember, we are earth
and to the earth we must return.[1]

Pentecost

While there are numerous themes that are part of the
Church's celebration of Pentecost Sunday, this might be an appropriate day to focus on the power of the Spirit to guide us in
the work of reclaiming the earth. Pentecost is the final day of
Easter, and Easter is the feast of resurrection. The resurrection
of Jesus is seen in the Scriptures as the beginning of the new
creation, so creation themes are appropriate in this season. The
origins of the feast of Pentecost lie in the Jewish feast of the
same name, originally a harvest feast that had become, by the
time of Christ, a feast of the covenant at Sinai. These multiple
themes of harvest, new creation, and covenant offer a variety
of ways of focusing on ecological themes.

Rituals for Outdoors

Throughout the Christian tradition of worship, there have
been numerous examples of rituals celebrated outdoors. The
blessing of fields and crops, the blessing of the fishing fleet,
the Easter Vigil bonfire, May processions, and rural life Masses
are just a few of these. While most of the Church's worship occurs within the worship space, parishes should be attentive to
occasions when rituals are appropriate outdoors. Such occasions will naturally remind us of the beauty of creation but
also may at times make us aware of the ecological damage
around us. Both can help motivate us to heal the earth.

Parish Community Gardens

Many city and suburban parishes have already found
ways to foster gardening, which helps us to stay in touch with
the earth and to feed people at the same time. Some parishes
have turned vacant parish land into community gardens for
those who do not have their own land to plant. Sometimes

1. *Maryknoll* 87:3 (March 1993) 1. Used with permission.

these gardens also supply food shelves or soup kitchens for the needy. Such efforts are to be commended and imitated.

Architecture Open to Nature

Those who are building or remodeling churches might be sensitive to the possibility of architecture that is open to nature. Some churches have clear windows behind the altar, providing a view of trees and flowers in season. Others have gathering spaces (vestibules) that lead to the main worship space with similar views of nature. Others have a garden as the backdrop for the reservation chapel.

Another way to link nature and worship is to arrange the entry to the church building through a garden area. Such a garden provides a touch of beauty and a bit of a buffer between the parking lot and the church. People often find this a help in making the transition from the rush of travel to the prayerfulness of worship. In good weather it also provides a good place for parishioners to socialize before and after worship.

Parish Conservation and Recycling

Parish communities, like all organizations, have a responsibility to foster conservation and recycling. This responsibility flows both from the parish's own use of resources and from the role of the parish as a witness to parishioners and to the wider community. How the parish handles trash at parish dinners, dances, and picnics speaks loudly to all present about responsible stewardship. Parish efforts to conserve energy in heating and cooling systems and in lighting patterns can prompt parishioners to do the same at home. Parish groups might work to help low-income families insulate their homes for energy conservation. Parish offices should arrange recycling of paper and other resources, and parish groups might sponsor recycling centers if the civic community has not yet done so. In a variety of ways, every parish can promote wise stewardship in the use of all the resources the earth provides.

Preaching on Ecology

There is a great need at this point in history to help people recognize their moral obligation to care for the environment as an important part of their Christian faith. This means that preaching should sometimes focus on this issue, so vital for the future of life on this planet. It would be irresponsible for preachers of the word to ignore this issue, to conduct worship as if the fate of the earth did not matter. To praise the Creator while ignoring the destruction of creation does not make sense.

Once again, care must be taken not to "use" the liturgy to promote a social agenda, but there is a valid way to bring these issues to the assembly's attention in preaching. The primary principle is that the homily should be based on the readings proclaimed from Scripture. Those who prepare worship should be alert to readings that invite an ecological focus for preaching.

The following are some examples of Sundays when the readings might support such preaching. It should be obvious that they vary in the degree to which they focus on ecological issues. Some weeks are clearly appropriate for a full homily on those issues, while other weeks only touch upon them and might simply suggest an example in the homily. Many of the readings focus on justice issues, which are crucial to moving toward harmony with all creation. The Scriptures themselves suggest many of the same connections between the various issues that affect the environment discussed above.

—*Second Sunday of Advent, Year A* (Isaiah 11:1-10): "He shall judge the poor with justice and decide aright for the land's afflicted. . . . the wolf shall be a guest of the lamb. . . . There shall be no harm or ruin on all my holy mountain." This vision of the prophet links justice and peace and harmony in creation. Note again the psalm response: "Justice shall flourish in his time, and fullness of peace forever."

—*Third Sunday of Advent, Year A* (Isaiah 35:1-6, 10): "The desert and the parched land will exult; the steppe will rejoice and bloom." The prophet sees the flowering of creation as a result of God's saving action. Note also the second reading (James 5:7-10): "See how the farmer awaits the precious yield of the soil," a passage that reminds us of the gift that the earth is.

—*First Sunday of Advent, Year B* (Isaiah 63:16-17, 19; 64:2-7): "All of us have become like unclean men; all our good deeds are like polluted rags. . . . we are the clay and you are the potter." This offers a good reminder of God's sovereignty and our need for salvation. Note also the refrain of the responsorial psalm: "Lord, make us turn to you, let us see your face and we shall be saved."

—*Second Sunday of Advent, Year B* (2 Peter 3:8-14): "What we await are new heavens and a new earth where . . . the justice of God will reside." This passage also links the need for justice with the future of creation.

—*Third Sunday of Advent, Year C* (Luke 3:10-18): "Let the man who has two coats give to him who has none. The man who has food should do the same." This call to share the world's goods has far-reaching applications.

All these Advent readings can be situated in the context of Advent longing for a savior. During this season we face the evils that still reign in our world and cry out to God for healing. Only when we know the power of evil in our lives do we really understand our need for a savior. Advent is a time to lament those facets of our life in which the kingdom has not yet come. Environmental destruction is certainly one of the evils we need to lament.

—*Feast of the Baptism of the Lord, Year A* (Isaiah 42:1-4, 6-7): "I, the Lord, have called you for the victory of justice." This passage calls for justice, a prerequisite for ending environmental degradation.

—*First Sunday of Lent, Year A* (Genesis 2:7-9; 3:1-7): The story of creation is an obvious basis for preaching on ecology. Note also the classic temptations in the gospel (Matthew 4:1-11): the lure of consumerism ("bread"), arrogance ("throw yourself down"), and power ("kingdoms") are the basis of much sin against the environment. The temptations are also recounted in Years B and C.

—*Third Sunday of Lent, Year A* (Exodus 17:3-7): The Lord provides water for the people in the desert. In the gospel (John 4:5-42), Jesus drinks from the well and promises living water.

—*First Sunday of Lent, Year B* (Genesis 9:8-15): The story of the flood speaks both of destruction and of preservation of all creatures.

—*Third Sunday of Lent, Year B* (Exodus 20:1-17): The commandments include several that apply to environmental questions: having other gods, killing, stealing, coveting. The gospel passage (John 2:13-25) might lead to reflection on how our greed destroys the temple of creation, too.

—*First Sunday of Lent, Year C* (Deuteronomy 26:4-10): This reading presents the fruits of the land as gifts of God to be shared.

—*Third Sunday of Lent, Year C* (Exodus 3:1-8, 13-15): God's presence in the burning bush might remind us of God's presence in all creation. Note also God's call to Moses to liberate the enslaved. The second reading (1 Corinthians 10:1-6, 10-12) also has words of warning that could be applied to environmental issues, and the gospel (Luke 13:1-9) also calls for reform.

—*Fourth Sunday of Lent, Year C* (Joshua 5:9, 10-12): The people eat of the produce of the land. In the gospel (Luke 15:1-3, 11-32), the prodigal son wastes his father's treasure, but he is still forgiven. This passage might give us hope despite our history of wastefulness.

—*Fifth Sunday of Lent, Year C* (Isaiah 43:16-21): This passage promises restoration of the land and of the people. Note the similar themes in Psalm 126, the responsorial psalm. The gospel (John 8:1-11) might even suggest our common guilt in damaging the environment.

These Lenten readings are part of the whole season devoted to repentance and renewal of our baptismal commitments. Sins against creation are one area that needs more attention in our penance services and general Lenten preaching.

—*Second Sunday of Easter, Year A and B* (Acts 2:42-47; Acts 4:32-35): Both of these passages show the early Christians sharing all things in common, a reminder that the earth's goods are given to all.

—*Third Sunday of Easter, Year A* (Luke 24:13-35): "They had come to know him in the breaking of the bread." Recognizing Christ's presence in the Eucharist should sensitize us to recognize the divine presence throughout creation.

—*Feast of the Ascension, Year A* (Ephesians 1:17-23): "He has put all things under Christ's feet and has made him thus exalted, head of the church, which is his body: the fullness of him who fills the universe in all its parts." This passage reminds us that Christ is present throughout creation, and it ought to foster respect for creation.

—*Vigil of Pentecost, Years ABC*: Three of the alternatives listed for the first reading offer ecological echoes: the passage from Genesis (11:1-9) prompts thoughts of the global cooperation necessary for progress (as does the first reading on Pentecost itself—Acts 2:1-11); the passage from Exodus (19:3-8, 16-20) reminds us of God's sovereignty ("all the earth is mine"); the passage from Ezekiel (37:1-14) speaks of dry bones living again. The second reading (Romans 8:22-27) also speaks of creation's hope for redemption.

—*Fourth Sunday of Easter, Year C* (Revelation 7:9, 14-17): This vision of heaven shows Christ the Shepherd providing food and life-giving water to his chosen ones, a vision to sustain our hope.

—*Fifth Sunday of Easter, Year C* (Revelation 21:1-5): John's vision of a new heaven and a new earth calls us to work to "make all things new." The gospel commandment of love of neighbor (John 13:31-33, 34-35) applies to ecological issues, as it does to so many issues.

These readings in the Easter season fit into the emphasis of the whole fifty-day feast. We celebrate the resurrection of Christ as the beginning of a new creation, and we reflect during this time, along with those newly baptized, on how new life in Christ is to be lived out in daily life. Certainly care for creation is part of the living out of our baptism.

—*Fourth Sunday in Ordinary Time, Year A* (Matthew 5:1-12): The beatitudes offer a lifestyle that would go a long way toward ending many of the causes of environmental degra-

dation. The other two readings (Zephaniah 2:3; 3:12-13 and
1 Corinthians 1:26-31) also call for humility, which would
counter the arrogance that has led to much destruction.

—*Fifth Sunday in Ordinary Time, Year A* (Isaiah 58:7-10): The
call to share the goods of the earth leads to a promise of a
brighter future.

—*Eighth Sunday in Ordinary Time, Year A* (Matthew 6:24-34):
This passage reminds us that accumulation of wealth is
not the goal of life, that God wills all people to have food
to eat and clothes to wear, and that all people are cherished in God's sight.

—*Ninth Sunday in Ordinary Time, Year A* (Matthew 7:21-27):
The parable about building one's house on a rock could
easily be applied to environmental practices. Note also
the words about blessing and curse in the first reading
(Deuteronomy 11:18, 26-28).

—*Fifteenth Sunday in Ordinary Time, Year A* (Isaiah 55:10-11 and
Matthew 13:1-23): Both passages relate seeds and yields
to our response to the word of God. It seems possible to
reverse the direction and ask how our hearing the word of
God leads us to care for seeds and crops.

—*Sixteenth Sunday in Ordinary Time, Year A* (Matthew 13:24-
43): Here is another text using images of planting, which
includes both good and evil seeds. Note also Wisdom's
acceptance of God's sovereignty and the call to repentance in the first reading (Wisdom 12:13, 16-19).

—*Eighteenth Sunday in Ordinary Time, Year A* (Isaiah 55:1-3 and
Matthew 14:13-21): Both passages speak of God providing
food for the crowds without cost. Proper distribution of
food remains a major challenge in our world today.

—*Nineteenth Sunday in Ordinary Time, Year A* (1 Kings 19:9, 11-
13 and Matthew 14:22-33): These two passages raise the
question of where we expect to find God—only in great
theophanies or also in the small things of life?

—*Twenty-Third Sunday in Ordinary Time, Year A* (Ezekiel 33:7-9;
Romans 13:8-10; Matthew 18:15-20): Ezekiel and Matthew
speak of admonishing the sinner, while Paul in the letter

to the Romans calls us to love of neighbor. All three passages might be related to confronting pollution and waste out of love for all people, present and future.

—*Twenty-Seventh Sunday in Ordinary Time, Year A* (Isaiah 5:1-7 and Matthew 21:33-43): Both selections focus on stewardship, a prime issue for ecology.

—*Twenty-Eighth Sunday in Ordinary Time, Year A* (Isaiah 25:6-10 and Philippians 4:12-14, 19–20): Isaiah's vision of the Lord's banquet is linked to God's removal of death from the earth. Paul thanks the Philippians for sharing their goods with him.

—*Thirty-Third Sunday in Ordinary Time, Year A* (Proverbs 31:10-13, 19-20, 30-31 and Matthew 25:14-30): Both passages praise good stewardship of what God has given us for life.

—*Feast of Christ the King, Year A* (Matthew 25:31-46): This picture of the last judgment calls for us to recognize Christ in all those in need.

—*Eleventh Sunday in Ordinary Time, Year B* (Ezekiel 17:22-24 and Mark 4:26-34): Both passages use nature images to speak of God's power to bring about change in the world.

—*Twelfth Sunday in Ordinary Time, Year B* (Job 38:1, 8-11 and Mark 4:35-41): Both of these texts remind us of God's sovereignty over nature. Note, too, Paul's words about a new creation in the second reading (2 Corinthians 5:14-17).

—*Thirteenth Sunday in Ordinary Time, Year B* (Wisdom 1:13-15; 2:23-24 and Mark 5:21-43): Wisdom speaks both of the inherent goodness of creation and of God's will for life. The gospel reminds us of God's power over life and death.

—*Seventeenth Sunday in Ordinary Time, Year B* (2 Kings 4:42-44 and John 6:1-15): These two miraculous multiplications of the loaves might prompt us to ask how we can find food to share with all.

—*Eighteenth Sunday in Ordinary Time, Year B* (Exodus 16:2-4, 12-15 and John 6:24-35): The manna in both passages was God's way of feeding God's people. How can we feed the world today?

—*Twenty-Third Sunday in Ordinary Time, Year B* (James 2:1-5): This passage challenges the unjust distribution of the world's goods that marks our own time so clearly.

—*Twenty-Fourth Sunday in Ordinary Time, Year B* (James 2:14-18): James calls for faith to act to meet the needs of the poor. Note also the gospel's call to deny ourselves (Mark 8:27-35).

—*Twenty-Fifth Sunday in Ordinary Time, Year B* (James 3:16—4:3): This passage focuses directly on the greed that leads to injustice and war. Peace and the preservation of the environment both require justice.

—*Twenty-Sixth Sunday in Ordinary Time, Year B* (James 5:1-6): Once again James chastises the rich for unjust practices.

—*Twenty-Eighth Sunday in Ordinary Time, Year B* (Wisdom 7:7-11 and Mark 10:17-30): Both passages suggest that there are things in life more important than wealth.

—*Thirty-Second Sunday in Ordinary Time, Year B* (1 Kings 17:10-16 and Mark 12:38-44): Both widows gave what they could not afford to share, a sharp rebuke to our greed and selfishness with the goods of the world.

—*Second Sunday in Ordinary Time, Year C* (John 2:1-12): The miracle at the wedding in Cana reminds us of how God works through created realities.

—*Third Sunday in Ordinary Time, Year C* (1 Corinthians 12:12-30): This passage is a classic text on the interconnectedness of members of Christ's body and the way our fate is linked to that of one another.

—*Sixth Sunday in Ordinary Time, Year C* (Luke 6:17, 20–26): This version of the beatitudes adds woes to those who are rich and full, perhaps a warning especially needed in the developed countries of the world.

—*Eighth Sunday in Ordinary Time, Year C* (Sirach 27:4-7 and Luke 6:39-45): Both of these texts speak of trees and fruit. While this is not exactly ecology, the need to examine all the results of our living is central to the passages and to ecological awareness.

—*Fifteenth Sunday in Ordinary Time, Year C* (Colossians 1:15-20): This text presents Christ as the source of creation and as the head of creation.

—*Eighteenth Sunday in Ordinary Time, Year C* (Ecclesiastes 1:2; 2:21-23 and Luke 12:13-21): The message of both passages reveals the folly of accumulating more and more, challenging our consumerism and greed.

—*Twenty-Fifth Sunday in Ordinary Time, Year C* (Amos 8:4-7 and Luke 16:1-13): Amos' condemnation of injustice is forceful, while Jesus reminds us that we cannot serve both God and money (greed).

—*Twenty-Sixth Sunday in Ordinary Time, Year C* (Amos 6:1, 4-7 and Luke 16:19-31): It is hard to imagine two stronger passages challenging the rich on their treatment of the poor.

—*Thirtieth Sunday in Ordinary Time, Year C* (Sirach 35:12-14, 16-18 and Luke 18:9-14): In the first reading Sirach promises that God will hear the lowly, and in the gospel Jesus calls us to humility. Both themes relate to ecological issues.

—*Thirty-First Sunday in Ordinary Time, Year C* (Wisdom 11:22—12:1): This selection makes clear God's love for all of creation and his preservation of it.

Questions for Reflection and Discussion

1. What is the first practical step you can take to improve your parish worship? What is the first step you can take to improve the care of the environment?

2. Can you think of times when the liturgy was misused to promote some cause? How did you react? Do you understand how liturgy teaches and forms us?

3. How well are symbols used in your parish worship? Which symbols are used well, and which are used poorly? What can be done to make better use of the symbols in worship, especially the central symbols of the sacraments?

4. Are any artificial materials used in your worship? What steps can be taken to replace them with authentic materials?

5. How can you celebrate the earth, water, and air in parish worship? Can you imagine a prayer service with this kind of focus? Would people come? Why or why not?

6. Does your parish celebrate Soil and Water Stewardship Week? If not, should you start? What about rural life Masses? Should city parishes celebrate these occasions, too?

7. How could the feast of St. Francis be more fully celebrated in your parish and/or in your home? Does your parish celebration of pro-life month include concerns for the environment?

8. Are environmental questions ever included in your parish penitential services? Would a separate penitential service focused on the environment be feasible, or should you include these issues in regular services?

9. Have you ever heard environmental issues included as part of the general intercessions at Mass? Can you try writing such petitions? How would you get them into your parish liturgy planning process?

10. Have you ever celebrated liturgy outdoors? When and why? How did you find the experience? What occasions might be appropriate for such liturgies?

11. How much is the natural world in evidence within and around your worship space? Can this be improved somehow?

12. How clear is the parish commitment to recycling? Do you recycle at home? Can you encourage recycling in your community?

13. Have you ever heard a homily that touched on environmental issues? What passages of Scripture speak to you about these issues? How can you encourage the preachers in your community to address these issues?

ABOUT THE AUTHOR:

Fr. Lawrence E. Mick has published five other books with The Liturgical Press: *To Live as We Worship, Understanding the Sacraments Today, Penance: The Once and Future Sacrament, RCIA: Renewing the Church as an Initiating Assembly,* and *Worshiping Well: A Mass Guide for Planners and Participants.* A priest of the Archdiocese of Cincinnati, he is a free-lance writer, speaker, and liturgical consultant.